Go Web Scraping Quick Start Guide

Implement the power of Go to scrape and crawl data
from the web

Vincent Smith

BIRMINGHAM - MUMBAI

Go Web Scraping Quick Start Guide

Copyright © 2019 Packt Publishing

Commissioning Editor: Pavan Ramchandani
Acquisition Editor: Aditi Gour
Content Development Editor: Smit Carvalho
Technical Editor: Surabhi Kulkarni
Copy Editor: Safis Editing
Project Coordinator: Pragati Shukla
Proofreader: Safis Editing
Indexer: Mariammal Chettiyar
Graphics: Alishon Mendonsa
Production Coordinator: Jyoti Chauhan

First published: January 2019

Production reference: 1290119

Published by Packt Publishing Ltd.
Livery Place
35 Livery Street
Birmingham
B3 2PB, UK.

ISBN 978-1-78961-570-8

www.packtpub.com

mapt.io

Mapt is an online digital library that gives you full access to over 5,000 books and videos, as well as industry leading tools to help you plan your personal development and advance your career. For more information, please visit our website.

Why subscribe?

- Spend less time learning and more time coding with practical eBooks and Videos from over 4,000 industry professionals

- Improve your learning with Skill Plans built especially for you

- Get a free eBook or video every month

- Mapt is fully searchable

- Copy and paste, print, and bookmark content

Packt.com

Did you know that Packt offers eBook versions of every book published, with PDF and ePub files available? You can upgrade to the eBook version at www.packt.com and as a print book customer, you are entitled to a discount on the eBook copy. Get in touch with us at customercare@packtpub.com for more details.

At www.packt.com, you can also read a collection of free technical articles, sign up for a range of free newsletters, and receive exclusive discounts and offers on Packt books and eBooks.

Contributors

About the author

Vincent Smith has been a software engineer for 10 years, having worked in various fields from health and IT to machine learning, and large-scale web scrapers. He has worked for both large-scale Fortune 500 companies and start-ups alike and has sharpened his skills from the best of both worlds. While obtaining a degree in electrical engineering, he learned the foundations of writing good code through his Java courses. These basics helped spur his career in software development early in his professional career in order to provide support for his team. He fell in love with the process of teaching computers how to behave and set him on the path he still walks today.

I would like to first and foremost thank my parents and my wife for supporting me in writing this book, and believing that I actually do have something to share. I would like to thank my co-workers, past and present, for being a shining example that impostor syndrome is all in your head and you should always share your knowledge. You were not born with your knowledge, so be the one that someone else can learn from.

About the reviewer

Ladjimi Chiheb Eddine is a professional Python/Django developer with extensive knowledge of Ethereum, Solidity, Golang, PostgreSQL, and Bitcoin. He is an open source enthusiast who is trying to help people in Stack Overflow and many QA forums by responding to their answers.

Currently, he resides in Paris, where he works as a senior Python/Django developer.

I would like to thank my family and all those who love me for their support over the years. Without them, I would not have been able to find the strength to continue my work and improve my skills.

Packt is searching for authors like you

If you're interested in becoming an author for Packt, please visit authors.packtpub.com and apply today. We have worked with thousands of developers and tech professionals, just like you, to help them share their insight with the global tech community. You can make a general application, apply for a specific hot topic that we are recruiting an author for, or submit your own idea.

Table of Contents

Preface

The internet is a place full of interesting information and insights just waiting to be gleaned. Much like golden nuggets, these fragmented pieces of data can be collected, filtered, combined, and refined to produce extremely valuable products. Armed with the right knowledge, skills, and a little creativity, you can build a web scraper that can power multi-billion-dollar companies. To support this, you need to use the best tools for the job, starting with a programming language built for speed, simplicity, and safety.

The Go programming language combines the best ideas from its predecessors and cutting-edge ideology, leaving out the unnecessary fluff, to produce a razor-sharp set of tools and clean architecture. With the Go standard library and projects from open source contributors, you have everything you need to build a web scraper of any size.

Who this book is for

This book is for anyone with a little coding experience who is curious about how to build a web scraper that is fast and efficient.

What this book covers

Chapter 1, *Introducing Web Scraping and Go*, explains what web scraping is and how to install the Go programming language and tools.

Chapter 2, *The Request/Response Cycle*, outlines the structure of HTTP requests and responses, and explains how to use Go to make and process them.

Chapter 3, *Web Scraping Etiquette*, explains how to build a web scraper that uses best practices and recommendations for crawling the web efficiently, while respecting others.

Chapter 4, *Parsing HTML*, shows how to use various tools to parse information from HTML pages.

Chapter 5, *Web Scraping Navigation*, demonstrates the best ways to navigate websites efficiently.

Chapter 6, *Protecting Your Web Scraper*, explains how to use various tools to navigate through the internet safely and securely.

Chapter 7, *Scraping with Concurrency*, introduces the Go concurrency model and explains how to build a productive web scraper.

Chapter 8, *Scraping at 100x*, provides a blueprint for building a large-scale web scraper and provides some examples from the open source community.

To get the most out of this book

In order to get the most from this book, you should familiarize yourself with your Terminal or Command Prompt, ensure you have a good internet connection, and read each chapter, even if you think you already know it. The readers of this book should keep an open mind as to how they think a web scraper should act, and they should learn the current best practices and proper etiquette. This book also focuses on the Go programming language, covering the installation, basic commands, the standard library, and package management, so some familiarity with Go will be helpful as this book covers the language in a broad sense and only goes into the depth that is needed for web scraping. To be able to run most of the code in this book, the reader should be familiar with their Terminal or Command Prompt in order to run the examples, among other tasks.

Download the example code files

You can download the example code files for this book from your account at www.packt.com. If you purchased this book elsewhere, you can visit www.packt.com/support and register to have the files emailed directly to you.

You can download the code files by following these steps:

1. Log in or register at www.packt.com
2. Select the **SUPPORT** tab
3. Click on **Code Downloads & Errata**
4. Enter the name of the book in the **Search** box and follow the onscreen instructions

Once the file is downloaded, please make sure that you unzip or extract the folder using the latest version of:

- WinRAR/7-Zip for Windows
- Zipeg/iZip/UnRarX for Mac
- 7-Zip/PeaZip for Linux

The code bundle for the book is also hosted on GitHub at `https://github.com/PacktPublishing/Go-Web-Scraping-Quick-Start-Guide`. In case there's an update to the code, it will be updated on the existing GitHub repository.

We also have other code bundles from our rich catalog of books and videos available at `https://github.com/PacktPublishing/`. Check them out!

Conventions used

There are a number of text conventions used throughout this book.

`CodeInText`: Indicates code words in text, database table names, folder names, filenames, file extensions, pathnames, dummy URLs, user input, and Twitter handles. Here is an example: "This is using the `net/http` package's default HTTP client to request the `index.html` resource."

A block of code is set as follows:

```
POST /login HTTP/1.1
Host: myprotectedsite.com
Content-Type: application/x-www-form-urlencoded
Content-Length: 38

username=myuser&password=supersecretpw
```

Any command-line input or output is written as follows:

```
go run main.go
```

Bold: Indicates a new term, an important word, or words that you see onscreen. For example, words in menus or dialog boxes appear in the text like this. Here is an example: "In this case, you will receive a status code of **500 Internal Server Error**."

 Warnings or important notes appear like this.

 Tips and tricks appear like this.

Get in touch

Feedback from our readers is always welcome.

General feedback: If you have questions about any aspect of this book, mention the book title in the subject of your message and email us at customercare@packtpub.com.

Errata: Although we have taken every care to ensure the accuracy of our content, mistakes do happen. If you have found a mistake in this book, we would be grateful if you would report this to us. Please visit www.packt.com/submit-errata, selecting your book, clicking on the Errata Submission Form link, and entering the details.

Piracy: If you come across any illegal copies of our works in any form on the Internet, we would be grateful if you would provide us with the location address or website name. Please contact us at copyright@packt.com with a link to the material.

If you are interested in becoming an author: If there is a topic that you have expertise in and you are interested in either writing or contributing to a book, please visit authors.packtpub.com.

Reviews

Please leave a review. Once you have read and used this book, why not leave a review on the site that you purchased it from? Potential readers can then see and use your unbiased opinion to make purchase decisions, we at Packt can understand what you think about our products, and our authors can see your feedback on their book. Thank you!

For more information about Packt, please visit packt.com.

Introducing Web Scraping and Go

1

Collecting, parsing, storing, and processing data are essential tasks that almost everybody will need to do in their software development career. Staying on top of emerging technologies that greatly improve the stability, speed, and efficiency of application development is another challenge. To provide insight into how to accomplish both of these goals, I have written this book. Here, you will find a guide for performing web scraping in Go. This book covers a broad perspective on web scraping, from the basics of the **Hypertext Transfer Protocol (HTTP)** and **Hypertext Markup Language (HTML)**, to building highly concurrent distributed systems.

In this chapter, you will find explanations on the following topics:

- What is web scraping?
- Why do you need a web scraper?
- What is Go?
- Why is Go a good fit for web scraping?
- How can you set up a Go development environment?

What is web scraping?

Web scraping at, its core, is collecting publicly available information from the internet for a specific purpose. It has taken form under many different names, such as following:

- Spiders
- Crawlers
- Bots

Although the name may carry a negative connotation, the practice of web scraping has been around since the beginning of the internet and has grown into various technologies and techniques. In fact, some companies have built their entire business on web scraping!

Why do you need a web scraper?

There are many different use cases where you might need to build a web scraper. All cases center around the fact that information on the internet is often disparate, but can be very valuable when collected into one single package. Often, in these cases, the person collecting the information does not have a working or business relationship with the producers of the data, meaning they cannot request the information to be packaged and delivered to them. Because of the lack of this relationship, the one who needs the data has to rely on their own means to gather the information.

Search engines

One well-known use case for web scraping is indexing websites for the purpose of building a search engine. In this case, a web scraper would visit different websites and follow references to other websites in order to discover all of the content available on the internet. By collecting some of the content from the pages, you could respond to search queries by matching the terms to the contents of the pages you have collected. You could also suggest similar pages if you track how pages are linked together, and rank the most important pages by the number of connections they have to other sites.

Googlebot is the most famous example of a web scraper used to build a search engine. It is the first step in building the search engine as it downloads, indexes, and ranks each page on a website. It will also follow links to other websites, which is how it is able to index a substantial portion of the internet. According to Googlebot's documentation, the scraper attempts to reach each web page every few seconds, which requires them to reach estimates of well into billions of pages per day!

If your goal is to build a search engine, albeit on a much smaller scale, you will find enough tools in this book to collect the information you need. This book will not, however, cover indexing and ranking pages to provide relevant search results.

Price comparison

Another known use case is to find specific products or services sold through various websites and track their prices. You would be able to see who sells the item, who has the lowest price, or when it is most likely to be in stock. You might even be interested in similar products from different sources. Having a web scraper periodically visit websites to monitor these products and services would be easily solve this problem. This is very similar to tracking prices for flights, hotels, and rental cars as well.

Sites like camelcamelcamel (`https://camelcamelcamel.com/`) build their business model around such a case. According to their blog post explaining how their system works, they actively collect pricing information from multiple retailers every half hour to every few hours, covering millions of products. This allows users to view pricing differences across multiple platforms, as well as get notified if the price of an item drops.

 You can read their post at `https://camelcamelcamel.com/blog/how-our-price-checking-system-works`.

This type of web scraper requires very careful parsing of the web pages to extract only the content that is relevant. In later chapters, you will learn how to extract information from HTML pages in order to collect this information.

Building datasets

Data scientists often need hundreds of thousands of data points in order to build, train, and test machine learning models. In some cases, this data is already pre-packaged and ready for consumption. Most of the time, the scientist would need to venture out on their own and build a custom dataset. This is often done by building a web scraper to collect raw data from various sources of interest, and refining it so it can be processed later on. These web scrapers also need to periodically collect fresh data to update their predictive models with the most relevant information.

A common use case that data scientists run into is determining how people feel about a specific subject, known as sentiment analysis. Through this process, a company could look for discussions surrounding one of their products, or their overall presence, and gather a general consensus. In order to do this, the model must be trained on what a positive comment and a negative comment are, which could take thousands of individual comments in order to make a well-balanced training set. Building a web scraper to collect comments from relevant forums, reviews, and social media sites would be helpful in constructing such a dataset.

These are just a few examples of web scrapers that drive large business such as Google, Mozenda, and `Cheapflights.com`. There are also companies that will scrape the web for whatever available data you need, for a fee. In order to run scrapers at such a large scale, you would need to use a language that is fast, scalable, and easy to maintain.

What is Go?

Go is a programming language created by Google employees in 2007. At the time of its creation, the goal was to build a language that was fast, safe, and simple. Go first officially released its 1.0 version in 2012 and is one of the fastest growing programming languages today. According to the *Stack Overflow 2018 Developer Survey*, Go is ranked in the top five of the most-loved languages and the top three in the most-wanted languages.

Go powers many large-scale web infrastructure platforms and tools such as Docker, Kubernetes, and Terraform. These platforms enable companies to build production-scale products supporting Fortune 500 companies. This is mostly the result of the design of the Go language, making it straightforward and clear to work with. Many other companies using Go for their development often tout the performance improvements over other languages.

Why is Go a good fit for web scraping?

The architecture of the Go programming language, as well as its standard libraries, make it a great choice for building web scrapers that are fast, scalable, and maintainable. Go is a statically typed, garbage-collected language with a syntax closer to C/C++. The syntax of the language will feel very familiar to developers coming from object-oriented programming languages. Go also has a few functional programming elements as well, such as higher-order functions. With all that being said, there are three main reasons why Go is a great fit for web scraping:

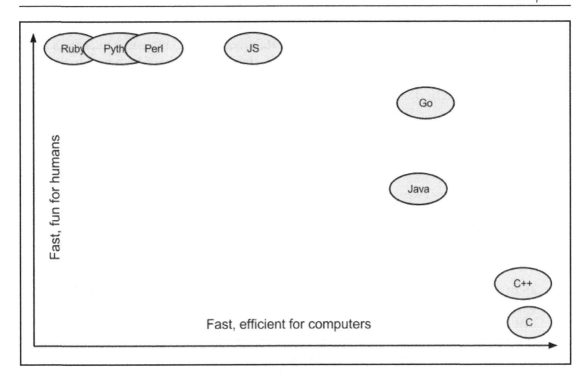

Go is fast

Speed is one of the primary objectives of the Go programming language. Many benchmarks put the speed of Go on par with that of C++, Java, and Rust, and miles ahead of languages such as Python and Ruby. Benchmark tests should always be considered with a bit of skepticism, but Go consistently stands out as a language with extremely high-performance numbers. This speed is typically coupled with a low resource footprint, as the runtime is very lightweight and does not use much RAM. One of the hidden benefits of this is being able to run Go programs on smaller machines, or to run multiple instances on the same machine, without significant overhead. This reduces the cost of operating a web scraper at larger scales.

This speed is inherently important in building web scrapers, and becomes more noticeable at larger scales. Take, for example, a web scraper that requires two minutes to scrape a page; you could theoretically process 720 pages in a day. If you were able to reduce that time to one minute per page, you would double the amount of pages per day to 1,440! Better yet, this would be done at the same cost. The speed and efficiency of Go allow you to do more with less.

Go is safe

One of the contributing factors to its speed is the fact that Go is statically typed. This makes the language ideal for building systems at a large scale and being confident in how your program will run in production. Also, since Go programs are built with a compiler instead of being run with an interpreter, it allows you to catch more bugs at compile time and greatly reduces the dreaded runtime errors.

This safety net is also extended to the Go garbage collector. Garbage collection means that you do not need to manually allocate and deallocate memory. This helps prevent memory leaks that might occur from mishandling objects in your code. Some may argue that garbage collection impedes the performance of your application, however, the Go garbage collector adds very little overhead in terms of interfering with your code execution. Many source report that the pauses caused by Go's garbage collector are less than one millisecond. In most cases, it's a very small price to pay to avoid chasing down memory leaks in the future. This certainly holds true for web scrapers.

As web scrapers grow in both size and complexity, it can be difficult to track all of the errors that may occur during processing. Thinking on the scale of processing thousands of web pages per day, one small bug could cause significantly affect the collection of data. At the end of the day, data missed is money lost, so preventing as many known errors as possible before the system is running is critical to your system.

Go is simple

Beyond the architecture of the Go programming language itself, the standard library offers all the right packages you need to make web scraping easy. Go offers a built-in HTTP client in the `net/http` package that is fully-featured out of the box, but also allows for a lot of customization. Making an HTTP request is as simple, as follows:

```
http.Get("http://example.com")
```

Also a part of the `net/http` package are utilities to structure HTTP requests, HTTP responses, and all of the HTTP status codes, which we will dive into later in this book. You will rarely need any third-party packages to handle communication with web servers. The Go standard library also has tools to help analyze HTTP requests, quickly consume HTTP response bodies, and debug the requests and responses in your web scraper. The HTTP client in the `net/http` package is also very configurable, letting you tune special parameters and methods to suit your specific needs. This typically will not need to be done, but the option exists if you encounter such a situation.

This simplicity will help eliminate some of the guesswork of writing code. You will not need to determine the best way to make an HTTP request; Go has already worked it out and provided you with the best tools you need to get the job done. Even when you need more than just the standard library, the Go community has built tools that follow the same culture of simplicity. This certainly makes integrating third-party libraries an easy task.

How to set up a Go development environment

Before you get started building a web scraper, you will need the proper tools. Setting up a development environment for writing Go code is relatively simple. There are not a lot of external tools that you will need to install, and there is support for all major computing platforms. For all of the tools listed in this chapter, you will find individual instructions for Windows, Mac, and Linux systems. Also, since all of the tools we will use are open source, you will be able to access the source code and build it for your specific needs if necessary.

Go language and tools

First and foremost, you'll need to install the Go programming language and tools on your machine. The installation process varies for different operating systems so please follow the instructions at `https://golang.org/doc/install`. On the installation page, you will find instructions for downloading Go for your platform, as well as the minimum operating system requirements.

It would be a good idea for you to spend some extra time browsing the Go programming language website to learn more about the language, read tutorials, and find the standard library documentation.

This is a screenshot from the installation page from the Go website, containing all of the instructions necessary for installing Go on your computer:

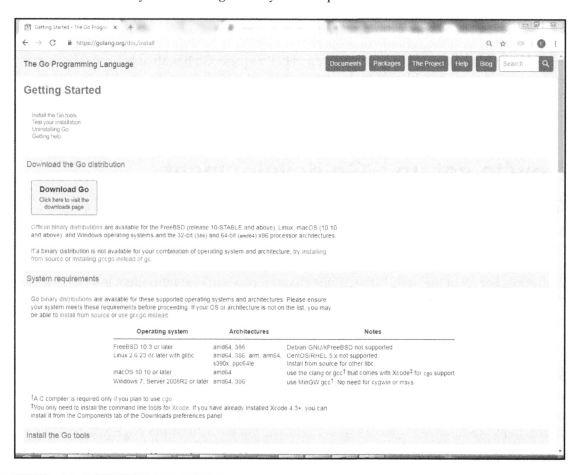

You can also build the language from source if you are so inclined. By the end of the installation, you should have the all of the Go libraries, the Go command line, and a simple hello world project built to ensure that everything was installed properly.

It is very important to follow the instructions all the way through testing your installation. Go can be a little tricky sometimes with respect to $GOPATH. Once you set up your $GOPATH, you must ensure that following is done:

- You have the required src, bin, and pkg directories
- All source code is contained within the src directory
- The folder structure inside your src directory mimics what you want your package names to be

By completing the testing section, you will save yourself a lot of frustration in the future.

 Since the release of version 1.11, the Go team has announced support for Go modules, which allows you to develop outside of the $GOPATH. Because this feature is still considered experimental, this book will continue with the classic method for Go development.

Git

You will also need to install the Git version control software. This will be used to download third-party libraries onto your machine. The go get command relies on Git being installed on your system to download libraries and install them directly into your $GOPATH. You may also feel free to use Git to download the examples for each chapter. All of the examples in this book will be using open source libraries that are available on GitHub. You can install Git for your system by following the instructions at https://git-scm.com/download.

 The Git command-line tool is a vast set of commands used for versioning, storing, and retrieving source code. These commands are the basis that power the GitHub website. It is highly recommended that you learn how to use the tool to interact with the GitHub site, rather than going through the UI.

The following is a screenshot of the Git download page, containing the links for your respective operating system:

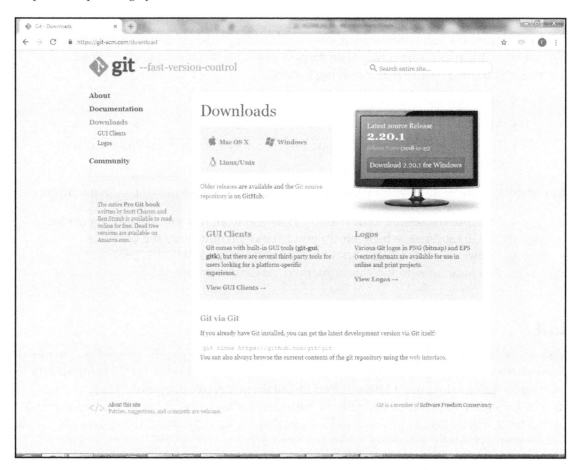

Editor

The second tool you will need is a good text editor or **Integrated Development Environment (IDE)**. If you are not familiar with IDEs, they are basically text editors that are custom-built for writing applications for specific programming languages. One well-known IDE for Go is GoLand by JetBrains. This comes with built-in support for syntax highlighting, run and debug modes, built-in version control, and package management.

GoLand is available as a 30-day trial, after which you must buy a license to continue using it.

The following is a screenshot of the GoLand IDE displaying the standard `Hello World` program:

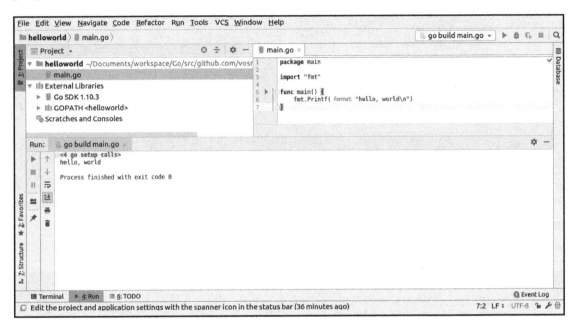

If you prefer to use a text editor, there are many available and they often have plugins for Go that make developing easier. Two of the best text editors available today are Visual Studio Code by Microsoft and Atom by GitHub. Both of these are general purpose editors that also have plugins for syntax highlighting, building, and running Go code. This way you can add what you need without too much overhead.

This screenshot is the same `Hello World` program, displayed in Visual Studio Code:

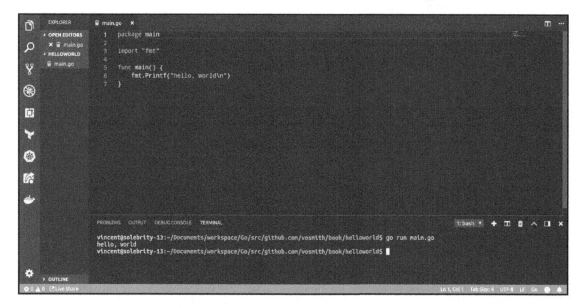

Finally, the Atom Version of the `Hello World` program looks like the following screenshot:

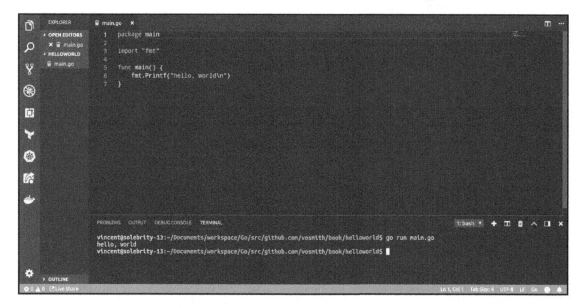

Both the Visual Studio Code and Atom are excellent choices for building Go applications due to the level of community support for the plugins, which I highly recommend installing. Alternatively, you can write Go programs in any text editor and run the code using your terminal or Command Prompt with the standard Go commands.

You will need a solid internet connection. A proper internet connection will eliminate errors connecting to different websites. If you are building a web scraper that sits behind a network firewall, or if you have a weak network connection, you may encounter difficulties accessing some of the sites used as examples in this book.

Summary

In this chapter, you learned a few of the use cases for building a web scraper and examples of businesses related to them. You also learned a few of the strengths of the Go programming language and created a development environment suitable for building your web scraper. These steps should help you get started on that path.

In Chapter 2, *The Request/Response Cycle*, we look at how to communicate with web servers in Go. We will learn the basics of how your web scraper communicates with web servers.

2
The Request/Response Cycle

Before you can build a web scraper, you must take a second and think about how the internet works. At its core, the internet is a network of computers connected together, discoverable through **Domain Lookup System** (**DNS**) servers. When you want to visit a website, your browser sends the website URL to a DNS server, the URL is translated into an IP address, and your browser then sends a request to the machine at that IP address. The machine, called a web server, receives and inspects the request, and makes a decision on what to send back to your browser. Your browser then parses the information sent by the server and displays content on your screen depending on the format of the data. The web server and browser are able to communicate because of the adherence to a global set of rules called the HTTP. In this chapter, you will learn some of the key points on the HTTP request and response cycle.

This chapter covers the following topics:

- What do HTTP requests look like?
- What do HTTP responses look like?
- What are HTTP status codes?
- What do HTTP requests/responses look like in Go?

What do HTTP requests look like?

When a client (such as a browser) requests a web page from a server, it sends an HTTP request. The format for such a request defines an action, a resource, and the Version of the HTTP protocol. Some HTTP requests include extra information for the server to process, such as a query or specific metadata. Depending on the action, you also may be sending the server new information for the server to process.

HTTP request methods

There are nine current HTTP request methods, which define a general action desired by the client. Each method carries a particular connotation as to how the server should process the request. The nine request methods are as follows:

- GET
- POST
- PUT
- DELETE
- HEAD
- CONNECT
- TRACE
- OPTIONS
- PATCH

The most common request methods that you will need are GET, POST, and PUT. GET requests are used for retrieving information from a website. POST and PUT requests are for sending information, such as user login data, to a website. These types of requests are usually sent only when submitting some type of form data, which we will cover in later chapters in this book.

In building a web scraper, the vast majority of the time you will be sending HTTP GET requests to a server in order to get a web page. The simplest example of a GET request for http://example.com/index.html looks something like this:

```
GET /index.html HTTP/1.1
Host: example.com
```

The client sends this message to the server with the GET action to obtain the index.html resource using the 1.1 Version of the HTTP protocol. This first line of an HTTP request is called the request line and is the core of an HTTP request.

HTTP headers

Below the request line are a series of key-value pairs that provide metadata describing how the request should be handled. These metadata fields are called HTTP headers. In our simple request, made earlier, we have a single HTTP header that defines the target host we are trying to reach. This information is not required by the HTTP protocol; however, it is almost always sent in order to provide clarification on who should be receiving the request.

If you were to inspect the HTTP request sent by your web browser, you would see many more HTTP headers. The following is an example sent by a Google Chrome browser to the same example.com website:

```
GET /index.html HTTP/1.1
Host: example.com
Connection: keep-alive
Cache-Control: max-age=0
Upgrade-Insecure-Requests: 1
User-Agent: Mozilla/5.0 (X11; Linux x86_64) AppleWebKit/537.36 (KHTML, like
Gecko) Chrome/69.0.3497.100 Safari/537.36
Accept:
text/html,application/xhtml+xml,application/xml;q=0.9,image/webp,image/apng
,*/*;q=0.8
Accept-Encoding: gzip, deflate
Accept-Language: en-US,en;q=0.9
If-None-Match: "1541025663+gzip"
If-Modified-Since: Fri, 09 Aug 2013 23:54:35 GMT
```

The basics of the HTTP request are the same, however, your browser provides significantly more request headers, mostly related to how to handle cached HTML pages. We will discuss some of these headers in more detail in the following chapters.

The server reads the request and processes all of the headers to decide how to respond to your request. In the most basic scenario, the server will respond saying **Your request is OK** and deliver the contents of index.html.

Query parameters

For some HTTP requests, extra information needs to be provided by the client in order to refine the request. This is usually done in two different ways. For HTTP GET requests, there is a defined way to include extra information in a request using the URL. Placing a ? at the end of a URL defines the end of the URL resource, and the next section defines query parameters. These parameters are key-value pairs defining the extra information sent to the server. The key value pairs are written as follows:

```
key1=value1&key2=value2&key3 ...
```

You will see this quite commonly when you are performing searches. As a hypothetical example, if you were on a site searching for shoes, you might encounter a paginated results page and the URL might look something like this:

```
https://buystuff.com/product_search?keyword=shoes&page=1
```

Notice that the resource is product_search, which is followed by the query parameters for the keyword and the page. This way, you can collect the products from all pages by adjusting the query.

Query parameters are defined by the website. There are no standard parameters that all websites must have, so it will take some investigation on your part depending on the site you are scraping.

Request body

Query parameters are typically only used on HTTP GET requests. For requests where you are sending data to the server, such as POST and PUT requests, you would send a request body that holds all of your extra information. Request bodies are placed after the HTTP headers in an HTTP request, with a one-line space between them. The following is a hypothetical POST request for logging into an imaginary website:

```
POST /login HTTP/1.1
Host: myprotectedsite.com
Content-Type: application/x-www-form-urlencoded
Content-Length: 38

username=myuser&password=supersecretpw
```

In this request, we are sending our `username` and `password` to `myprotectedsite.com/login`. The headers for this request must describe the request body so the server is able to process it. In this case, we declare that the request body be in the `x-www-form-urlencoded` format, which is the same format used for the query parameters in the *Query parameters* section. We could use alternative formats, such as `JSON` or `XML` or even plain text, but only if it is supported by the server. The `x-www-form-urlencoded` format is the most widely supported and is generally a safe bet. The second parameter we define in the header is the length of the request body in bytes. This allows the server to efficiently prepare for processing the data, or rejecting the request completely if it is too large.

The Go standard library has good support for building HTTP requests quite simply—if you are familiar with the structure, at least. We will revisit how this is done later in this chapter.

What do HTTP responses look like?

When the server responds to your request, it will provide a status code, some response headers, and the content of the resource in most cases. Staying with our previous request for `http://www.example.com/index.html`, you will be able to see what a typical response looks like, section by section.

Status line

The first line of an HTTP response is called the status line and typically looks like this:

```
HTTP/1.1 200 OK
```

First, it tells you what Version of the HTTP protocol the server is using. This should always match the version sent by the client HTTP request. In this case, our server is using version `1.1`. The next portion is the HTTP status code. This is code used to indicate the status of the response. Most of the time, you should see a status code of **200**, indicating that the request was successful and a response body will follow. This is not always the case, and we will look deeper into HTTP status codes in the next section. The **OK** is a human-readable description of the status code, which is only used for your own reference.

Response headers

HTTP response headers follow the status line and look very similar to HTTP request headers. These also provide metadata specific to the response, much like request headers do. Here are the headers from our example.com response:

```
Accept-Ranges: bytes
Cache-Control: max-age=604800
Content-Type: text/html; charset=UTF-8
Date: Mon, 29 Oct 2018 13:31:23 GMT
Etag: "1541025663"
Expires: Mon, 05 Nov 2018 13:31:23 GMT
Last-Modified: Fri, 09 Aug 2013 23:54:35 GMT
Server: ECS (dca/53DB)
Vary: Accept-Encoding
X-Cache: HIT
Content-Length: 1270
```

In this response, you can see some headers describing the content of the page, how to cache it, and the size of the remaining data. This information is useful for processing the data after it has been received.

Response body

The rest of the response is the actual web page that renders index.html. Your browser would take this and draw the text, images, and styling for the web page itself, but for the purpose of scraping, it is not necessary. An abbreviated version of the response body looks similar to this:

```
<!doctype html>
<html>
<head>
 <title>Example Domain</title>
 <meta charset="utf-8" />
 <meta http-equiv="Content-type" content="text/html; charset=utf-8" />
 <meta name="viewport" content="width=device-width, initial-scale=1" />
 <!-- The <style> section was removed for brevity -->
</head>
<body>
 <div>
  <h1>Example Domain</h1>
<p>This domain is established to be used for illustrative examples in
    documents. You may use this domain in examples without prior
    coordination or asking for permission.</p>
<p><a href="http://www.iana.org/domains/example">More
```

```
information...</a></p>
 </div>
</body>
</html>
```

The majority of the time, you will be handling responses from a web server that has a status code of **200**, meaning that the request was OK. However, from time to time, you will encounter other status codes that your web scraper should be aware of.

What are HTTP status codes?

HTTP status codes are used to inform the HTTP client of the status of the HTTP request. In some cases, the HTTP server needs to inform the client that the request was not understood, or that extra actions need to be taken in order to get a full response. The HTTP status codes are divided into four separate ranges, each one covering a specific type of response.

100–199 range

These codes are used to provide information to the HTTP client on how to deliver a request. These codes are usually processed by the HTTP client itself and will be handled before your web scraper needs to worry about them.

For example, the client may prefer that requests be sent using the HTTP 2.0 protocol and request the server to change. If the server can support HTTP 2.0, it will respond with a status code of **101**, meaning switching protocols. A case like this would be handled by the client under the hood, so you need not to be concerned about it.

200–299 range

The 200-299 range of status codes indicates that the request was successfully processed with no issues. The most important code to note here is a status code of **200**. This means you have a response body coming your way and everything was perfect!

In some cases, you might be downloading chunks of a large file (think on the scale of gigabytes) where you are requesting ranges of bytes to download from the server. In this case, a successful response should be a **206**, meaning the server is returning partial content from the original file.

Other codes in this range indicate that the request was successful but the server is processing information in the background, or there is no content at all. These are not typically seen in web scraping.

300–399 range

If you encounter a status code in this range, it means that the request is understood but extra steps are necessary to get to the actual content. The most common cases you will run into here are for redirection.

The **301, 302, 307,** and **308** status codes all indicate that the resource you are looking for can be found at another location. In the header for this response, the server should indicate where the final location in the response header is. For example, a **301** response might look like this:

```
HTTP/1.1 301 Moved Permanently
Location: /blogs/index.html
Content-Length: 190

<html>
<head><title>301 Moved Permanently</title></head>
<body bgcolor="white">
<h1>301 Moved Permanently</h1>
Please go to <a href="/blogs/index.html">/blogs/index.html</a>
</body>
</html>
```

The server includes a `Location` header telling the client where the location of the resource was moved to, and that the client should send the next request to that location. The content here can be ignored in most cases.

Other status codes in this range are related to the use of proxies and cached information, both of which we will discuss in future chapters.

400–499 range

When you encounter status codes in this range, you should be concerned. The `400` range indicates that there was something wrong with your request. There are many different issues that can trigger these responses, such as poor formatting, authentication issues, or unusual requests. Servers send these codes back to their clients to tell them that they will not fulfill the request because something looks sketchy.

One status code you may already be familiar with is **404 Not Found**. This occurs when your request a resource that the server cannot seem to find. This could be due to a misspelling of the resource or because the page does not exist at all. Sometimes, websites update files on their servers and possibly forget to update the links in the web pages with their new locations. This can cause **broken links**, and it is especially common when a page links to an external website.

Other common status codes in this range that you may encounter are **401 Unauthorized** and **403 Forbidden**. In both cases, this means that you are trying to access pages that require proper authentication credentials. There are many different forms of authentication for the web, and this book will cover only the basics in the future chapters.

The last status code that I would like to highlight in this range is **429 Too Many Requests**. Some web servers are configured with rate limits, meaning that you can only maintain a certain number of requests over a certain period of time. If you are surpassing this rate, then you are not only putting unreasonable stress on the web server, but you are also exposing your web scraper, which puts it at risk for being blacklisted. Following the proper web scraping etiquette is beneficial for both you and your target website.

500–599 range

Status codes in this range usually represent errors pertaining to the server itself. Although these errors are usually not your fault, you will still need to be aware of them and adapt to the situation.

The status codes **502 Bad Gateway** and **503 Service Temporarily Unavailable** indicate that the server was unable to produce the resource due to a problem within the server. This does not necessarily mean that the resource does not exist, or that you are not allowed to access it. When you encounter these codes, it is best to put the request aside and try again later. If you are seeing these codes often, you may want to stop all requests and allow the server to address its issues.

There are cases where something in the web server breaks for no particular reason. In this case, you will receive a status code of **500 Internal Server Error**. These errors are generic and are often the cause of a crash in the server code. The same advice for retrying your request, or having your scraper back off, are also relevant in this case.

What do HTTP requests/responses look like in Go?

Now that you are familiar with the basics of HTTP requests and responses, it's time to see what this looks like in Go. The standard library in Go provides a package named `net/http`, which contains all of the tools you will need to build a client that is capable of requesting pages from web servers and processing the responses with very little effort.

Let's take a look at the example from the beginning of this chapter, where we were accessing the web page at `http://www.example.com/index.html`. The underlying HTTP request instructs the web server at `example.com` to `GET` the `index.html` resource:

```
GET /index.html HTTP/1.1
Host: example.com
```

Using the Go `net/http` package, you would use the following line of code:

```
r, err := http.Get("http://www.example.com/index.html")
```

 The Go programming language allows for multiple variables to be returned from a single function. This is also how errors are typically thrown and handled.

This is using the `net/http` package's default HTTP client to request the `index.html` resource, which returns two objects: the HTTP response (`r`) and an error (`err`). In Go, errors are returned as values, instead of being thrown and caught by other code. If the `err` is equal to `nil`, then we know there were no issues communicating with the web server.

Let's look at the response from the beginning of this chapter. If the request were successful, the server would return something like this:

```
HTTP/1.1 200 OK
Accept-Ranges: bytes
Cache-Control: max-age=604800
Content-Type: text/html; charset=UTF-8
Date: Mon, 29 Oct 2018 13:31:23 GMT
Etag: "1541025663"
Expires: Mon, 05 Nov 2018 13:31:23 GMT
Last-Modified: Fri, 09 Aug 2013 23:54:35 GMT
Server: ECS (dca/53DB)
Vary: Accept-Encoding
X-Cache: HIT
Content-Length: 1270
```

```
<!doctype html>
<html>
<head>
 <title>Example Domain</title>
 <meta charset="utf-8" />
 <meta http-equiv="Content-type" content="text/html; charset=utf-8" />
 <meta name="viewport" content="width=device-width, initial-scale=1" />
 <!-- The <style> section was removed for brevity -->
</head>
<body>
 <div>
 <h1>Example Domain</h1>
 <p>This domain is established to be used for illustrative examples in
    documents. You may use this
    domain in examples without prior coordination or asking for
    permission.</p>
 <p><a href="http://www.iana.org/domains/example">More
information...</a></p>
 </div>
</body>
</html>
```

All of this information is contained in the r variable, which is a *http.Response that was
returned from the http.Get() function. Let's take a look at the definition of what an
http.Response object looks like in Go. The following struct is defined in the Go
standard library:

```
type Response struct {
    Status string
    StatusCode int
    Proto string
    ProtoMajor int
    ProtoMinor int
    Header Header
    Body io.ReadCloser
    ContentLength int64
    TransferEncoding []string
    Close bool
    Uncompressed bool
    Trailer Header
    Request *Request
    TLS *tls.ConnectionState
}
```

The http.Response object contains all of the fields you need to process an HTTP response. Most notably, the StatusCode, Header, and Body would be useful in scraping. Let's put the request and response together in a simple example that saves the index.html file to your computer.

A simple request example

Inside the $GOPATH/src folder that you set up, create a folder called simplerequest. Inside simplerequest, create a file called main.go. Set the contents of main.go to be the following code:

```
package main

import (
 "log"
 "net/http"
 "os"
)

func main() {
 // Create the variables for the response and error
 var r *http.Response
 var err error

 // Request index.html from example.com
 r, err = http.Get("http://www.example.com/index.html")

 // If there is a problem accessing the server, kill the program and print
the error the console
 if err != nil {
  panic(err)
 }

 // Check the status code returned by the server
 if r.StatusCode == 200 {
  // The request was successful!
  var webPageContent []byte

  // We know the size of the response is 1270 from the previous example
  var bodyLength int = 1270

  // Initialize the byte array to the size of the data
  webPageContent = make([]byte, bodyLength)

  // Read the data from the server
```

```
r.Body.Read(webPageContent)

// Open a writable file on your computer (create if it does not
    exist)
var out *os.File
out, err = os.OpenFile("index.html", os.O_CREATE|os.O_WRONLY, 0664)

if err != nil {
 panic(err)
}

// Write the contents to a file
out.Write(webPageContent)
out.Close()
} else {
 log.Fatal("Failed to retrieve the webpage. Received status code",
 r.Status)
}
}
```

The example given here is a little verbose in order to show you the basics of Go programming. As you progress through the book, you will be introduced to tips and tricks to make your code more succinct.

You can run this code from inside the `simplerequest` folder by typing following command inside of a terminal window:

go run main.go

If all goes well, you should not see messages printed, and there should be a new file called `index.html` containing the contents of the response body. You can even open the file with a web browser!

With these basics in mind, you should be on your way to creating a web scraper in Go that can create HTTP requests and read HTTP responses with just a few lines of code.

Summary

In this chapter, we covered the basic formats of HTTP requests and responses. We also saw how HTTP requests are made in Go, as well as how the `http.Response` struct relates to real HTTP responses. Finally, we created a small program that sent an HTTP response to `http://www.example.com/index.html` and processed the HTTP response. For the full HTTP specification, I encourage you to visit `https://www.w3.org/Protocols/`.

In `Chapter 3`, *Web Scraping Etiquette,* we look at the best practices for being a good citizen of the web.

3
Web Scraping Etiquette

Before jumping into too much code, there are a few points you will need to keep in mind as you begin running a web scraper. It is important to remember that we all must be good citizens of the internet in order for everyone to get along. Keeping that in mind, there are many tools and best practices to follow in order to ensure that you are being fair and respectful when adding a load to an outside web server. Stepping outside of these guidelines could put your scraper at risk of being blocked by the web server, or in extreme cases, you could find yourself in legal trouble.

In this chapter, we will cover the following topics:

- What is a robots.txt file?
- What is a User-Agent string?
- How can you throttle your web scraper?
- How do you use caching?

What is a robots.txt file?

Most of the pages on a website are free to be accessed by web scrapers and bots. Some of the reasons for allowing this are in order to be indexed by search engines or to allow pages to be discovered by content curators. Googlebot is one of the tools that most websites would be more than happy to give access to their content. However, there are some sites that may not want everything to show up in a Google search result. Imagine if you could google a person and instantly obtain all of their social media profiles, complete with contact information and address. This would be bad news for the person, and certainly not a good privacy policy for the company hosting the site. In order to control access to different parts of a website, you would configure a `robots.txt` file.

The `robots.txt` file is typically hosted at the root of the website in the `/robots.txt` resource. This file contains definitions of who can access which pages in this website. This is done by describing a bot that matches a `User-Agent` string, and specifying which paths are allowed and disallowed. Wildcards are also supported in the `Allow` and `Disallow` statements. The following is an example `robots.txt` file from Twitter:

```
User-agent: *
Disallow: /
```

This is the most restrictive `robots.txt` file you will encounter. It states that no web scraper can access any part of `twitter.com`. Violating this will put your scraper at risk of being blacklisted by Twitter's servers. On the other hand, websites like Medium are a little more permissive. Here is their `robots.txt` file:

```
User-Agent: *
Disallow: /m/
Disallow: /me/
Disallow: /@me$
Disallow: /@me/
Disallow: /*/edit$
Disallow: /*/*/edit$
Allow: /_/
Allow: /_/api/users/*/meta
Allow: /_/api/users/*/profile/stream
Allow: /_/api/posts/*/responses
Allow: /_/api/posts/*/responsesStream
Allow: /_/api/posts/*/related
Sitemap: https://medium.com/sitemap/sitemap.xml
```

Looking into this, you can see that editing profiles is disallowed by the following directives:

- `Disallow: /*/edit$`
- `Disallow: /*/*/edit$`

The pages that are related to logging in and signing up, which could be used for automated account creation, are also disallowed by `Disallow: /m/`.

If you value your scraper, do not access these pages. The `Allow` statements provide explicit permission to paths in the in `/_/` routes, as well as some `api` related resources. Outside of what is defined here, if there is no explicit `Disallow` statement, then your scraper has permission to access the information. In the case of Medium, this includes all of the publicly available articles, as well as public information about the authors and publications. This `robots.txt` file also includes a `sitemap`, which is an XML-encoded file listing all of the pages available on the website. You can think of this as a giant index, which can come in very handy.

One more example of a `robots.txt` file shows how a site defines rules for different `User-Agent` instances. The following `robots.txt` file is from Adidas:

```
User-agent: *
Disallow: /*null*
Disallow: /*Cart-MiniAddProduct
Disallow: /jp/apps/shoplocator*
Disallow: /com/apps/claimfreedom*
Disallow: /us/help-topics-affiliates.html
Disallow: /on/Demandware.store/Sites-adidas-US-Site/en_US/
User-Agent: bingbot
Crawl-delay: 1
Sitemap:
https://www.adidas.com/on/demandware.static/-/Sites-CustomerFileStore/defau
lt/adidas-US/en_US/sitemaps/adidas-US-sitemap.xml
Sitemap:
https://www.adidas.com/on/demandware.static/-/Sites-CustomerFileStore/defau
lt/adidas-MLT/en_PT/sitemaps/adidas-MLT-sitemap.xml
```

This example explicitly disallows access to a few paths for all web scrapers, as well as a special note for `bingbot`. The `bingbot` must respect the `Crawl-delay` of 1 second, meaning it cannot access any pages more than once per second. `Crawl-delays` are very important to take note of, as they will define how quickly you can make web requests. Violating this may generate more errors for your web scraper, or it may be permanently blocked.

What is a User-Agent string?

When an HTTP client makes a request to a web server, they identify who they are. This holds true for web scrapers and normal browsers alike. Have you ever wondered why a website knows that you are a Windows or a Mac user? This information is contained inside your `User-Agent` string. Here is an example `User-Agent` string for a Firefox browser on a Linux computer:

```
Mozilla/5.0 (X11; Linux x86_64; rv:57.0) Gecko/20100101 Firefox/57.0
```

You can see that this string identifies the family, name, and version of the web browser, as well as the operating system. This string will be sent with every request from this browser inside of a request header, such as the following:

```
GET /index.html HTTP/1.1
Host: example.com
User-Agent: Mozilla/5.0 (X11; Linux x86_64; rv:57.0) Gecko/20100101
Firefox/57.0
```

Not all `User-Agent` strings contain this much information. HTTP clients that are not web browsers are typically much smaller. Here are some examples:

- cURL: `curl/7.47.0`
- Go: `Go-http-client/1.1`
- Java: `Apache-HttpClient/4.5.2`
- Googlebot (for images): `Googlebot-Image/1.0`

`User-Agent` strings are a good way of introducing your bot and taking responsibility for following the rules set in a `robots.txt` file. By using this mechanism, you will be held accountable for any violations.

Example

There are open source tools available that help parse `robots.txt` files and validate website URLs against them to see if you have access or not. One project that I would recommend is available on GitHub called `robotstxt` by user `temoto`. In order to download this library, run the following command in your terminal:

```
go get github.com/temoto/robotstxt
```

The $GOPATH referred to here is the one you set up during the installation of the Go programming language back in Chapter 1, *Introducing Web Scraping and Go*. This is the directory with the src/ bin/ and pkg/ directories.

This will install the library on your machine at $GOPATH/src/github/temoto/robotstxt. If you would like, you can read the code to see how it all works. For the sake of this book, we will just be using the library in our own project. Inside your $GOPATH/src folder, create a new folder called robotsexample. Create a main.go file inside the robotsexample folder. The following code for main.go shows you a simple example of how to use the temoto/robotstxt package:

```go
package main

import (
  "net/http"

  "github.com/temoto/robotstxt"
)

func main() {
  // Get the contents of robots.txt from packtpub.com
  resp, err := http.Get("https://www.packtpub.com/robots.txt")
  if err != nil {
    panic(err)
  }
  // Process the response using temoto/robotstxt
  data, err := robotstxt.FromResponse(resp)
  if err != nil {
    panic(err)
  }
  // Look for the definition in the robots.txt file that matches the
default Go User-Agent string
  grp := data.FindGroup("Go-http-client/1.1")
  if grp != nil {
    testUrls := []string{
      // These paths are all permissable
      "/all",
      "/all?search=Go",
      "/bundles",

      // These paths are not
      "/contact/",
      "/search/",
      "/user/password/",
    }
```

```
    for _, url := range testUrls {
      print("checking " + url + "...")

      // Test the path against the User-Agent group
      if grp.Test(url) == true {
        println("OK")
      } else {
        println("X")
      }
    }
  }
}
```

 This example uses Go for each loop using the `range` operator. The `range` operator returns two variables, the first is the `index` of the `iteration` (which we ignore by assigning it to _), and the second is the value at that index.

This code checks six different paths against the `robots.txt` file for `https://www.packtpub.com/`, using the default `User-Agent` string for the Go HTTP client. If the `User-Agent` is allowed to access a page, then the `Test()` method returns `true`. If it returns `false`, then your scraper should not access this section of the website.

How to throttle your scraper

Part of good web scraping etiquette is making sure you are not putting too much load on your target web server. This means limiting the number of requests you make within a certain period of time. For smaller servers, this is especially true, as they have a much more limited pool of resources. As a good rule of thumb, you should only access the same web page as often as you think it will change. For example, if you were looking at daily deals, you would probably only need to scrape once per day. As for scraping multiple pages from the same website, you should first follow the `Crawl-Delay` in a `robots.txt` file. If there is no `Crawl-Delay` specified, then you should manually delay your requests by one second after every page.

There are many different ways to incorporate delays into your crawler, from manually putting your program to sleep to using external queues and worker threads. This section will explain a few basic techniques. We will revisit more complicated examples when we discuss the Go programming language concurrency model.

The simplest way to add throttle to your web scraper is to track the timestamps for requests that are made, and ensure that the elapsed time is greater than your desired rate. For example, if you were to scrape at a rate of one page per 5 seconds, it would look something like this:

```go
package main

import (
  "fmt"
  "net/http"
  "time"
)

func main() {
  // Tracks the timestamp of the last request to the webserver
  var lastRequestTime time.Time

  // The maximum number of requests we will make to the webserver
  maximumNumberOfRequests := 5

  // Our scrape rate at 1 page per 5 seconds
  pageDelay := 5 * time.Second

  for i := 0; i < maximumNumberOfRequests; i++ {
    // Calculate the time difference since our last request
    elapsedTime := time.Now().Sub(lastRequestTime)
    fmt.Printf("Elapsed Time: %.2f (s)\n", elapsedTime.Seconds())
    //Check if there has been enough time
    if elapsedTime < pageDelay {
      // Sleep the difference between the pageDelay and elapsedTime
      var timeDiff time.Duration = pageDelay - elapsedTime
      fmt.Printf("Sleeping for %.2f (s)\n", timeDiff.Seconds())
      time.Sleep(pageDelay - elapsedTime)
    }

    // Just for this example, we are not processing the response
    println("GET example.com/index.html")
    _, err := http.Get("http://www.example.com/index.html")
    if err != nil {
      panic(err)
    }

    // Update the last request time
    lastRequestTime = time.Now()
  }
}
```

> This example has many instances of : = when defining variables. This is a shorthand way, in Go, of simultaneously declaring and instantiating variables. It replaces the need to say the following:
>
> ```
> var a string
> a = "value"
> ```
>
> Instead, it becomes:
> ```
> a := "value"
> ```

In this example, we make requests to `http://www.example.com/index.html` once every five seconds. We know how long it has been since our last request, as we update the `lastRequestTime` variable and check it before we make each request. This is all you need to scrape a single website, even if you were scraping multiple pages.

If you were scraping multiple websites, you would need to separate `lastRequestTime` into one variable per website. The simplest way to do this would be with a `map`, Go's key-value structure, where the key would be the host and the value would be the timestamp for the last request. This would replace the definition with something like this:

```
var lastRequestMap map[string]time.Time = map[string]time.Time{
  "example.com": time.Time{},
  "packtpub.com": time.Time{},
}
```

Our `for` loop would also change slightly and set the value of the map to the current scrape time, but only for the website, we are scraping. For example, if we were to scrape the pages in an alternating manner, it might look something like this:

```
// Check if "i" is an even number
if i%2 == 0 {
  // Use the Packt Publishing site and elapsed time
  webpage = packtPage
  elapsedTime = time.Now().Sub(lastRequestMap["packtpub.com"])
} else {
  // Use the example.com elapsed time
  elapsedTime = time.Now().Sub(lastRequestMap["example.com"])
}
```

Finally, to update the map with the last known request time, we would use a similar block:

```
// Update the last request time
if i%2 == 0 {
  // Use the Packt Publishing elapsed time
  lastRequestMap["packtpub.com"] = time.Now()
} else {
```

```
    // Use the example.com elapsed time
    lastRequestMap["example.com"] = time.Now()
}
```

 You can find the full source code for this example on GitHub.

If you look at the output in the terminal, you will see that the first requests to either site have no delay and each sleep period is slightly less than five seconds now. This shows that the crawler is respecting each site's rate independently.

How to use caching

One last technique that can benefit your scraper, as well as reducing load on the website, is by only requesting new content when it changes. If your scraper is downloading the same old content from a web server, then you aren't getting any new information and the web server is doing unnecessary work. For this reason, most web servers implement techniques to provide the client with instructions on caching.

A website that supports caching, will give the client information on what it can store, and how long to store it. This is done through response headers such as `Cache-Control`, `Etag`, `Date`, `Expires`, and `Vary`. Your web scraper should be aware of these directives to avoid making unnecessary requests to the web server, saving you, and the server, time and computing resources. Let's take a look at our `http://www.example.com/index.html` response one more time, given as follows:

```
HTTP/1.1 200 OK
Accept-Ranges: bytes
Cache-Control: max-age=604800
Content-Type: text/html; charset=UTF-8
Date: Mon, 29 Oct 2018 13:31:23 GMT
Etag: "1541025663"
Expires: Mon, 05 Nov 2018 13:31:23 GMT
Last-Modified: Fri, 09 Aug 2013 23:54:35 GMT
Server: ECS (dca/53DB)
Vary: Accept-Encoding
X-Cache: HIT
Content-Length: 1270
...
```

The body of the response is not included in this example.

There are a few response headers used to communicate caching instructions that you should follow in order to increase the efficiency of your web scraper. These headers will inform you of what information to cache, for how long, and a few other helpful pieces of information to make life easier.

Cache-Control

The `Cache-Control` header is used to indicate whether this content is cacheable, and for how long. Some of the common values for this header are as follows:

- `no-cache`
- `no-store`
- `must-revalidated`
- `max-age=<seconds>`
- `public`

Cache directives such as `no-cache`, `no-store`, and `must-revalidate` exist to prevent the client from caching the response. Sometimes, the server is aware that the content on this page changes frequently, or is dependent on a source outside of its control. If none of these directives are sent, you should be able to cache the response using the provided `max-age` directive. This defines the number of seconds you should consider this content as fresh. After this time, the response is said to be stale and a new request should be made to the server.

In the response from the previous example, the server sends a `Cache-Control` header:

```
Cache-Control: max-age=604800
```

This indicates that you should cache this page for up to 604880 seconds (seven days).

Expires

The `Expires` header is another way of defining how long to retain cached information. This header defines an exact date and time from which the content will be considered stale and should be refreshed. This time should coincide with the `max-age` directive from the `Cache-Control` header, if one is provided.

In our example, the `Expires` header matches the 7-day expiration based on the `Date` header, which defines when the request was received by the server:

```
Date: Mon, 29 Oct 2018 13:31:23 GMT
Expires: Mon, 05 Nov 2018 13:31:23 GMT
```

Etag

The `Etag` is also important in keeping cached information. This is a key unique to this page, and will only change if the content of the page changes. After the cache expires, you can use this tag to check with the server if there is actually new content, without downloading a fresh copy. This works by sending an `If-None-Match` header containing the `Etag` value. When this happens, the server will check if the `Etag` on the current resource matches the `Etag` in the `If-None-Match` header. If it does match, then there have been no updates and the server responds with a status code of **304 Not Modified**, with some headers to extend your cache. The following is an example of a `304` response:

```
HTTP/1.1 304 Not Modified
Accept-Ranges: bytes
Cache-Control: max-age=604800
Date: Fri, 02 Nov 2018 14:37:16 GMT
Etag: "1541025663"
Expires: Fri, 09 Nov 2018 14:37:16 GMT
Last-Modified: Fri, 09 Aug 2013 23:54:35 GMT
Server: ECS (dca/53DB)
Vary: Accept-Encoding
X-Cache: HIT
```

The server, in this case, validates the `Etag` and provides a new `Expires` time, still matching the `max-age`, from the time this second request was fulfilled. This way, you still save time by not needing to read more data over the network. You can still use your cached pages to fulfill your needs.

Caching content in Go

The storage and retrieval of cached pages can be implemented by hand using your local filesystem, or a database to hold the data and the cached information. There are also open source tools available to help simplify this technique. One such project is httpcache by GitHub user gregjones.

The httpcache follows the caching requirements set by the **Internet Engineering Task Force (IETF)**, the governing body for internet standards. The library provides a module that can store and retrieve web pages from your local machine, as well as a plugin for the Go HTTP client to automatically handle all cache-related HTTP request and response headers. It also provides multiple storage backends where you can store the cached information, such as Redis, Memcached, and LevelDB. This will allow you to run a web scraper on different machines, but connect to the same cached information.

 As your scraper grows in size and you need to design a distributed architecture, a feature like this will be critical to ensure that time and resources are not wasted on duplicated work. Stable communication between all of your scrapers is key!

Let's take a look at an example using httpcache. First, install httpcache by typing the following commands into your terminal, shown as follows:

- go get github.com/gregjones/httpcache
- go get github.com/peterbourgon/diskv

 The diskv project is used by httpcache to store the web page on your local machine.

Inside your $GOPATH/src, create a folder called cache with a main.go inside it. Use the following code for your main.go file:

```
package main

import (
  "io/ioutil"

  "github.com/gregjones/httpcache"
  "github.com/gregjones/httpcache/diskcache"
)

func main() {
```

```
// Set up the local disk cache
storage := diskcache.New("./cache")
cache := httpcache.NewTransport(storage)

// Set this to true to inform us if the responses are being read from a
cache
cache.MarkCachedResponses = true
cachedClient := cache.Client()

// Make the initial request
println("Caching: http://www.example.com/index.html")
resp, err := cachedClient.Get("http://www.example.com/index.html")
if err != nil {
  panic(err)
}

// httpcache requires you to read the body in order to cache the response
ioutil.ReadAll(resp.Body)
resp.Body.Close()

// Request index.html again
println("Requesting: http://www.example.com/index.html")
resp, err = cachedClient.Get("http://www.example.com/index.html")
if err != nil {
  panic(err)
}

// Look for the flag added by httpcache to show the result is read from
the cache
_, ok = resp.Header["X-From-Cache"]
if ok {
  println("Result was pulled from the cache!")
}
}
```

This program uses the local disk cache to store the response from http://www.example.com/index.html. Under the hood, it reads all of the cache-related headers to determine if it can store the page and includes the expiration date with the data. On the second request, httpcache checks if the content is expired and returns the cached data instead of making another HTTP request. It also adds an extra header, X-From-Cache, to indicate that this is being read from the cache. If the page had expired, it would make the HTTP request with the If-None-Match header and handle the response, including updating the cache in case of a **304 Not Modified** response.

Using a client that is automatically set up to handle caching content will make your scraper run faster, as well as reducing the likelihood that your web scraper will be flagged as a bad citizen. When this is done in combination with respecting a website's `robots.txt` file and properly throttling your requests, you can scrape confidently, knowing that you are a respectable member of the web community.

Summary

In this chapter, you learned the basic etiquette for respectfully crawling the web. You learned what a `robots.txt` file is and why it is important to obey it. You also learned how to properly represent yourself using `User-Agent` strings. Controlling your scraper via throttling and caching was also covered. With these skills, you are one step closer to building a fully functional web scraper.

In `Chapter 4`, *Parsing HTML*, we will look at how to extract information from HTML pages using various techniques.

4
Parsing HTML

In the previous chapters, we have dealt with whole web pages, which is not really practical for most web scrapers. Although it is nice to have all of the content from a web page, most of the time, you will only need small pieces of information from each page. In order to extract this information, you must learn to parse the standard formats of the web, the most common of these being HTML.

This chapter will cover the following topics:

- What is the HTML format
- Searching using the strings package
- Searching using the regexp package
- Searching using XPath queries
- Searching using Cascading Style Sheets selectors

What is the HTML format?

HTML is the standard format used to provide web page context. An HTML page defines which elements a browser should draw, the content and style of the elements, and how the page should respond to interactions from the user. Looking back at our http://example. com/index.html response, you can see the following, which is what an HTML document looks like:

```
<!doctype html>
<html>
<head>
  <title>Example Domain</title>
  <meta charset="utf-8" />
  <meta http-equiv="Content-type" content="text/html; charset=utf-8" />
  <meta name="viewport" content="width=device-width, initial-scale=1" />
  <!-- The <style> section was removed for brevity -->
</head>
<body>
```

```
<div>
  <h1>Example Domain</h1>
  <p>This domain is established to be used for illustrative examples
      in documents. You may use this domain in examples without prior
      coordination or asking for permission.</p>
  <p><a href="http://www.iana.org/domains/example">More
      information...</a></p>
</div>
</body>
</html>
```

Files that adhere to the HTML specification follow a strict set of rules that define the syntax and structure of the document. By learning these rules, you can quickly and easily retrieve any information from any web page.

Syntax

HTML documents define elements of a web page by using tags with element names. Tags are always surrounded by angle brackets, such as the `<body>` tag. Each element defines the end of a tag set by using a forward slash before the tag name, such as `</body>`. The contents of the element lie between a set of opening and closing tags. For example, everything between the `<body>`, and matching `</body>` tag, defines the content of the body element.

Some tags also have extra properties defined in key-value pairs called attributes. These are used to describe extra information about the element. In the example shown, there is an `<a>` tag that has an attribute called `href`, whose value is `https://www.iana.org/domains/example`. In this case, the `href` is a property of the `<a>` tag and tells the browser that this element links to the URL provided. We'll look deeper into navigating these links in a later chapter.

Structure

Each HTML document has a specific layout starting with the `<!doctype>` tag. This tag is used to define the version of the HTML specification used to validate this specific document. In our case, the `<!doctype html>` refers to the HTML 5 specification. You may sometimes see tags such as this:

```
<!DOCTYPE HTML PUBLIC "-//W3C//DTD HTML 4.01//EN" "http://www.w3.org/TR/
html4/strict.dtd">
```

This would describe an `HTML 4.01` (strict) web page that follows definitions provided at the URL provided. We will not go into using the provided definition to validate the page in this book, as it is usually not necessary to do so.

Following the `<!doctype>` tag is the `<html>` tag, which holds the actual content of the web page. Inside the `<html>` tag, you will find the `<head>` and `<body>` tags for the document. The `<head>` tag contains metadata about the page itself, such as the title, as well as external files to include for building the web page. These files may be for styling, or for describing how elements react to user interactions.

 On the actual web page at `http://example.com/index.html`, you can see the `<style>` tag used to describe the sizes, colors, fonts, and spacing for various types of elements on the web page. This information was removed from the HTML document in this book to preserve space.

The `<body>` tag contains the bulk of the data that you will be interested in scraping. Inside the `<body>` element, you will find all of the text, images, videos, and links containing information for your web scraping needs. Collecting the data you need from the web page can be done in many different ways; you will see some of the common ways in the following sections.

Searching using the strings package

The most basic way to search for content is to use the `strings` package from the Go standard library. The `strings` package allows you to perform various operations on String objects, including searching for matches, counting occurrences, and splitting strings into arrays. The utility of this package can cover some use cases that you may run into.

Example – Counting links

One quick and easy piece of information that we could extract using the `strings` package is to count the number of links that are contained in a web page. The `strings` package has a function called `Count()`, which returns the number of times a substring occurs in a string. As we have seen before, links are contained in `<a>` tags. By counting the number of occurrences of `"<a"`, we can get a general idea of the number of links in a page. An example would look like the one given here:

```
package main

import (
```

```
      "fmt"
      "io/ioutil"
      "net/http"
      "strings"
  )

  func main() {
    resp, err := http.Get("https://www.packtpub.com/")
    if err != nil {
      panic(err)
    }

    data, err := ioutil.ReadAll(resp.Body)
    if err != nil {
      panic(err)
    }

    stringBody := string(data)

    numLinks := strings.Count(stringBody, "<a")
    fmt.Printf("Packt Publishing homepage has %d links!\n", numLinks)
  }
```

In this example, the `Count()` function is used to find the number of occurrences of "`<a`" in the home page for the Packt Publishing website.

Example – Doctype check

Another useful method in the `strings` package is the `Contains()` method. This is used to check for the existence of a substring in a string. For example, you could check for the HTML Version used to build a web page similar to the one given here:

```
  package main

  import (
    "io/ioutil"
    "net/http"
    "strings"
  )

  func main() {
    resp, err := http.Get("https://www.packtpub.com/")
    if err != nil {
      panic(err)
    }
```

```
data, err := ioutil.ReadAll(resp.Body)
if err != nil {
  panic(err)
}

stringBody := strings.ToLower(string(data))

if strings.Contains(stringBody, "<!doctype html>") {
  println("This webpage is HTML5")
} else if strings.Contains(stringBody, "html/strict.dtd") {
  println("This webpage is HTML4 (Strict)")
} else if strings.Contains(stringBody, "html/loose.dtd") {
  println("This webpage is HTML4 (Tranistional)")
} else if strings.Contains(stringBody, "html/frameset.dtd") {
  println("This webpage is HTML4 (Frameset)")
} else {
  println("Could not determine doctype!")
}
}
```

This example looks for information contained in a `<!doctype>` tag to check if it contains certain indicators for the HTML Version. Running this code will show you that the home page for Packt Publishing is built to the HTML 5 specification.

Relying on the `strings` package can reveal some very light information about a web page, but it does have its shortcomings. In both of the previous examples, the matches could be misleading if there are sentences in the document that contain the strings in unexpected places. Over generalizing a string search can lead to misinformation that can be avoided using more robust tools.

Searching using the regexp package

The `regexp` package in the Go standard library provides a deeper level of search by using regular expressions. This defines a syntax that allows you to search for strings in more complex terms, as well as retrieving strings from a document. By using capture groups in regular expressions, you can extract data matching a query from the web page. Here are a few useful tasks that the `regexp` package can help you achieve.

Example – Finding links

In the previous section, we used the `strings` package to count the number of links on a page. By using the `regexp` package, we can take this example further and retrieve the actual links with the following regular expression:

```
<a.*href\s*=\s*["'](http[s]{0,1}:\/\/.[^\s]*)["'].*>
```

This query should match any string that looks like a URL, inside an `href` attribute, inside of `<a>` tags.

The following program prints all of the links on the Packt Publishing home page. This same technique could be used to collect all of the images using querying for the `src` attributes of `<img>` tags:

```go
package main

import (
  "fmt"
  "io/ioutil"
  "net/http"
      "regexp"
)

func main() {
  resp, err := http.Get("https://www.packtpub.com/")
  if err != nil {
    panic(err)
  }

  data, err := ioutil.ReadAll(resp.Body)
  if err != nil {
    panic(err)
  }

  stringBody := string(data)

      re :=
regexp.MustCompile(`<a.*href\s*=\s*["'](http[s]{0,1}:\/\/.[^\s]*)["'].*>`)
      linkMatches := re.FindAllStringSubmatch(stringBody, -1)

      fmt.Printf("Found %d links:\n", len(linkMatches))
      for _,linkGroup := range(linkMatches){
          println(linkGroup[1])
      }
}
```

Example – Finding prices

Regular expressions can also be used to find content displayed on the web page itself. For example, you may be trying to find the price of an item. Let's look at the following example that shows the price of the *Hands-On Go Programming* book from Packt Publishing's website:

```go
package main

import (
  "fmt"
  "io/ioutil"
  "net/http"
      "regexp"
)

func main() {
  resp, err :=
http.Get("https://www.packtpub.com/application-development/hands-go-program
ming")
  if err != nil {
    panic(err)
  }

  data, err := ioutil.ReadAll(resp.Body)
  if err != nil {
    panic(err)
  }

  stringBody := string(data)

  re := regexp.MustCompile(`.*main-book-price.*\n.*(\$[0-9]*\.[0-9]{0,2})`)
  priceMatches := re.FindStringSubmatch(stringBody)

  fmt.Printf("Book Price: %s\n", priceMatches[1])
}
```

This program looks for a text string matching `main-book-price`, then looks for a USD-formatted decimal on the following line.

You can see that regular expressions can be used to extract strings in a document where the `strings` package is used mostly for discovering strings. Both of these techniques suffer from the same issue: you might match strings in unexpected places. In order to have a more fine-grained approach, the search needs to be more structured.

Searching using XPath queries

In the previous examples for parsing HTML documents, we treated HTML simply as searchable text, where you can discover information by looking for specific strings. Fortunately, HTML documents actually have a structure. You can see that each set of tags can be viewed as some object, called a node, which can, in turn, contain more nodes. This creates a hierarchy of root, parent, and child nodes, providing a structured document. In particular, HTML documents are very similar to XML documents, although they are not fully XML-compliant. Because of this XML-like structure, we can search for content in the pages using XPath queries.

XPath queries define a way to traverse the hierarchy of nodes in an XML document, and return matching elements. In our previous examples, where we were looking for <a> tags in order to count and retrieve links, we needed to search for the tags by string. This method can be problematic if similar matching strings are found in unexpected places in an HTML document, such as in a code comment or escaped text. If we use XPath queries such as //a/@href, we can traverse the HTML document structure for the actual <a> tag node and retrieve the href attribute.

Example – Daily deals

Using a structured querying language like XPath, you can easily collect unformatted data as well. In our previous examples, we've mostly looked at the prices of products. Prices are simpler to deal with because they generally follow a specific format. For example, you can use regular expressions to look for a dollar sign, followed by a one or more digits, a period, and two more digits. On the other hand, if you wanted to retrieve a block or multiple blocks of text where the content had no format, it would become more difficult to do so with basic string searches. XPath simplifies this by allowing you to retrieve all of the text content inside of a node.

The Go standard library has basic support for the handling of XML documents and elements; unfortunately, there is no XPath support. However, the open source community has built various XPath libraries for Go. The one I would recommend is htmlquery by GitHub user antchfx.

You can obtain this library by using the following command:

```
go get github.com/antchfx/htmlquery
```

The following example demonstrates how you can scrape daily deals using an XPath query to discover some basic product information:

```go
package main

import (
  "regexp"
  "strings"

  "github.com/antchfx/htmlquery"
)

func main() {
  doc, err :=
htmlquery.LoadURL("https://www.packtpub.com/packt/offers/free-learning")
  if err != nil {
    panic(err)
  }

  dealTextNodes := htmlquery.Find(doc, `//div[@class="dotd-main-book-
summary float-left"]//text()`)

  if err != nil {
    panic(err)
  }

  println("Here is the free book of the day!")
  println("--------------------------------")

  for _, node := range dealTextNodes {
    text := strings.TrimSpace(node.Data)
    matchTagNames, _ := regexp.Compile("^(div|span|h2|br|ul|li)$")
    text = matchTagNames.ReplaceAllString(text,"")
    if text != "" {
      println(text)
    }
  }
}
```

This program selects any `text()` found in the `div` element containing a `class` attribute, with the matching value of `dotd-main-book-summary`. This query also returns the names of the nodes that are children of targeted `div` elements, for example, `div` and `h2`, as well as empty text nodes. For this reason, we drop any known HTML tags (using a regular expression) and only print the remaining text nodes that are not empty strings.

Example – Collecting products

In this example, we will use an XPath query to retrieve the latest releases from the Packt Publishing website. On this web page, there are a series of `<div>` tags that contain more `<div>` tags, which will eventually lead to our information. Each of these `<div>` tags hold an attribute called `class`, which describes what the purpose of the node is. In particular, we are concerned with the `landing-page-row` class. The book-related `<div>` tags within the `landing-page-row` class have an attribute called `itemtype`, which tells us that the `div` is for a book and should contain other attributes holding the names and prices. It would not be possible to achieve this with the `strings` package, and a regular expression would be very laborious to design.

Let's take a look at the following example:

```go
package main

import (
  "fmt"
  "strconv"

  "github.com/antchfx/htmlquery"
)

func main() {
  doc, err := htmlquery.LoadURL("https://www.packtpub.com/latest-
  releases")
  if err != nil {
    panic(err)
  }

  nodes := htmlquery.Find(doc, `//div[@class="landing-page-row
  cf"]/div[@itemtype="http://schema.org/Product"]`)
  if err != nil {
    panic(err)
  }

  println("Here are the latest releases!")
  println("----------------------------")

  for _, node := range nodes {
    var title string
    var price float64

    for _, attribute := range node.Attr {
      switch attribute.Key {
      case "data-product-title":
```

```
      title = attribute.Val
    case "data-product-price":
      price, err = strconv.ParseFloat(attribute.Val, 64)
      if err != nil {
        println("Failed to parse price")
      }
    }
  }
}
  fmt.Printf("%s ($%0.2f)\n", title, price)
}
}
```

Using an XPath query that directly targets the elements in the document directly, we are able to navigate to the exact attribute of the exact node to retrieve the name and price of each of the books.

Searching using Cascading Style Sheets selectors

You can see how using a structured query language makes searching for, and retrieving, information much easier than basic string searches. However, XPath was designed for generic XML documents, not HTML. There is another structured query language that is made specifically for HTML. **Cascading Style Sheets (CSS)** were created to provide a way to add stylistic elements to HTML pages. In a CSS file, you would define a path to an element or multiple elements, and what describes the appearance. The definitions for the path to the element are called CSS selectors and are written specifically for HTML documents.

CSS selectors understand common attributes that we could use in searching HTML documents. In the previous XPath examples, we often used a query such as div[@class="some-class"] in order to search for elements with the class name some-class. CSS selectors offer a shorthand for class attributes by simply using a .. The same XPath query would look like div.some-class as a CSS query. Another common shorthand used here is searching elements with an id attribute, which is represented in CSS as a # symbol. In order to find an element with the id of main-body, you would use div#main-body as a CSS selector. There are many other niceties in the CSS selector specification that expand what can be done via XPath, as well as simplifying common queries.

Although there is no support for CSS selectors in the Go standard library, once again, the open source community has many tools that provide this functionality, the best of which is `goquery` by GitHub user `PuerkitoBio`.

You can obtain the library by using the following command:

```
go get github.com/PuerkitoBio/goquery
```

Example – Daily deals

The following examples will refine the XPath example, using `goquery` in place of `htmlquery`:

```
package main

import (
  "fmt"
  "strconv"

  "github.com/PuerkitoBio/goquery"
)

func main() {
  doc, err := goquery.NewDocument("https://www.packtpub.com/latest-
  releases")
  if err != nil {
    panic(err)
  }

  println("Here are the latest releases!")
  println("---------------------------")
  doc.Find(`div.landing-page-row div[itemtype$="/Product"]`).
    Each(func(i int, e *goquery.Selection) {
      var title string
      var price float64
      title,_ = e.Attr("data-product-title")
      priceString, _ := e.Attr("data-product-price")
      price, err = strconv.ParseFloat(priceString, 64)
      if err != nil {
        println("Failed to parse price")
      }
      fmt.Printf("%s ($%0.2f)\n", title, price)
    })
}
```

Using `goquery`, the search for the daily deals becomes much more succinct. In this query, we use one of the helper features that CSS selectors offer by using the `$=` operator. Instead of looking for the `itemtype` attribute, matching the exact string `http://schema.org/Product`, we can simply match the string that *ends with* `/Product`. We also use the `.` operator to look for the `landing-page-row` class. One key difference to note between this example and the XPath example is that you do not need to match the entire value of the class attribute. When we were searching with XPath, we had to use `@class="landing-page-row cf"` as a query. In CSS, is it not necessary to have exact matches for classes. As long as the element contains the `landing-page-row class`, it matches.

Example – Collecting products

In the code given here, you can see the CSS selector version of the collecting products example:

```
package main

import (
  "bufio"
  "strings"

  "github.com/PuerkitoBio/goquery"
)

func main() {
  doc, err :=
goquery.NewDocument("https://www.packtpub.com/packt/offers/free-learning")
  if err != nil {
    panic(err)
  }

  println("Here is the free book of the day!")
  println("--------------------------------")
  rawText := doc.Find(`div.dotd-main-book-summary div:not(.eighteen-days-countdown-bar)`).Text()
  reader := bufio.NewReader(strings.NewReader(rawText))

  var line []byte
  for err == nil{
    line, _, err = reader.ReadLine()
    trimmedLine := strings.TrimSpace(string(line))
    if trimmedLine != "" {
      println(trimmedLine)
```

```
        }
      }
    }
```

In this example, you can use CSS queries to return all of the text from all of the child elements as well. We use the `:not()` operator to exclude the countdown timer, and finally, to process the lines of text to ignore spaces and blank lines.

Summary

You can see that there are various ways of extracting data from HTML pages using different tools. Basic string searches and `regex` searches can collect information using very simple techniques, but there are cases where more structured query languages are needed. XPath provides great searching capabilities by assuming the document is XML-formatted and can cover generic searches. CSS selectors are the simplest way to search for and extract data from HTML documents and provide many helpful features that are HTML-specific.

In `Chapter 5`, *Web Scraping Navigation*, we will look at the best ways to crawl the internet efficiently and safely.

5
Web Scraping Navigation

So far, this book has focused on retrieving information for a single web page. Although this is the basis of web scraping, it does not cover the majority of use cases. More than likely, you will need to visit multiple web pages, or websites, in order to collect all of the information to fulfill your needs. This may entail visiting many known websites directly via a list or URLs, or following links discovered in some pages to more unknown places. There are many different ways of navigating your scraper through the web.

In this chapter, we will cover the following topics:

- How to follow links
- How to submit forms with POST requests
- How to track your history to avoid loops
- The difference between breadth-first and depth-first crawling

Following links

As you have seen in many examples throughout this book, there are HTML elements denoted by <a> tags that contain href attributes that reference different URLs. These tags, called anchor tags, are how links are generated on a web page. In a web browser, these links would typically have a different font color, often blue, with an underline. As a user in a web browser, if you wanted to follow a link, you would usually just click on it and you would be redirected to the URL. As a web scraper, the clicking action is usually not necessary. Instead, you can send a GET request to the URL in the href attribute itself.

If you find that the href attribute lacks the http:// or https:// prefix and the hostname, you must use the prefix and hostname of the current web page.

Example – Daily deals

In Chapter 4, *Parsing HTML*, we used an example where we retrieved the titles and the prices of the latest releases from the Packt Publishing website. You could collect more information about each book by following each link to the book's main web page. In the following code example, we will add the navigation to make this possible:

```go
package main

import (
  "fmt"
  "strings"
  "time"
  "github.com/PuerkitoBio/goquery"
)

func main() {
  doc, err :=
goquery.NewDocument("https://www.packtpub.com/latest-releases")
  if err != nil {
    panic(err)
  }

  println("Here are the latest releases!")
  println("---------------------------")
  time.Sleep(1 * time.Second)
  doc.Find(`div.landing-page-row div[itemtype$="/Product"] a`).
    Each(func(i int, e *goquery.Selection) {
      var title, description, author, price string
      link, _ := e.Attr("href")
      link = "https://www.packtpub.com" + link

      bookPage, err := goquery.NewDocument(link)
      if err != nil {
        panic(err)
      }
      title = bookPage.Find("div.book-top-block-info h1").Text()
      description = strings.TrimSpace(bookPage.Find("div.book-top-
      block-info div.book-top-block-info-one-liner").Text())
```

```
price = strings.TrimSpace(bookPage.Find("div.book-top-block-info
div.onlyDesktop div.book-top-pricing-main-ebook-price").Text())
authorNodes := bookPage.Find("div.book-top-block-info div.book-
top-block-info-authors")
 if len(authorNodes.Nodes) < 1 {
   return
 }
author = strings.TrimSpace(authorNodes.Nodes[0].FirstChild.Data)
fmt.Printf("%s\nby: %s\n%s\n%s\n--------------------\n\n",
title, author, price, description)
time.Sleep(1 * time.Second)
})
}
```

As you can see, we have modified the `Each()` loop to extract the link for every product listed in the web page. Each link only contains the relative path to the book, so we prefix the `https://www.packtpub.com` string to each link. Next, we navigate to the page itself by using the link we constructed, and scrape the desired information. At the end of each page, we sleep for 1 second so that our web scraper does not overburden the servers, observing the good etiquette we learned in `Chapter 3`, *Web Scraping Etiquette*.

Submitting forms

Up until this point, we have been able to request information from servers using only HTTP `GET` requests. These requests cover the vast majority of web scraping tasks that you will encounter as you build your own web scraper. However, there will come a time where you may need to submit some kind of form data in order to retrieve the information you are looking for. This form data could entail search queries, or a login screen, or any page that would require you to type into a box and click a **Submit** button.

For simple websites, this is done using an HTML `<form>` element, containing one or more `<input>` elements and a **Submit** button. This `<form>` element usually has attributes defining the `action` (where to send the `<form>` data), and a `method` (the HTTP method to use). By default, the web page will use an HTTP `GET` request to send the form data, but it is very common to see HTTP `POST` requests as well.

Example – Submitting searches

In the following example, you will see how to simulate a form submission by using the properties and elements of an HTML form. We will use the form located at the `https://hub.packtpub.com/` website to discover articles written about the Go programming language (commonly referred to as GoLang). On the home page of `https://hub.packtpub.com`, there is a search box in the top-left corner of the page, as shown in the following screenshot:

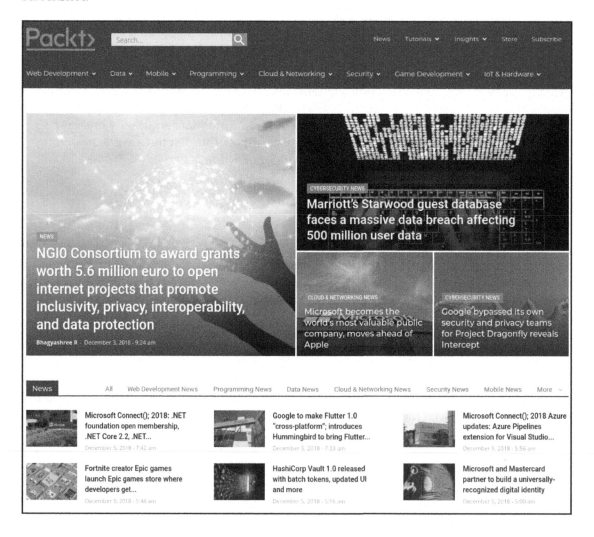

By right-clicking on the **Search...** box, you should be able to inspect the element using your browser's **Developer tools**. This reveals the HTML source code for the page, showing that this box is located in an HTML form. In Google Chrome, it looks similar to the following screenshot:

```
▼<form method="get" class="td-search-form" action="https://hub.packtpub.com/">
  ▼<div role="search" class="td-head-form-search-wrap">
    <input id="td-header-search" type="text" value name="s" autocomplete="off" placeholder="Search...">
    ▼<button class="mobile-search-form-btn" type="submit" id="td-header-search-top" value>
      ▼<i class="td-icon-search">
        ::before
      </i>
    </button>
  </div>
</form>
```

This form uses the HTTP GET method, and submits to the `https://hub.packtpub.com/` endpoint. The values for this form are taken from the `<input>` tags using the `name` attribute as a key, and the text within the Search box as the value. Because this form uses GET as a method, the key-value pairs are sent to the server as the query part of the URL. For our example, we want to submit GoLang as our search query. To do this, when you click the button to submit your query, your browser will send a GET request to `https://hub.packtpub.com/?s=Golang`.

The resulting page will contain all articles related to Go. You could scrape the title, dates, authors, and so on in order to keep an index of Go articles. By submitting this query periodically, you could discover new articles as soon as they are released.

Example – POST method

The form we used in the previous example used GET as a method. Hypothetically, if it were to use the POST method, there would be a slight difference in how the form is submitted. Instead of putting the values in the URL, you would need to build a request body instead. In the following example, the same form and search query will be structured as a POST request:

```
package main

import (
    "net/http"
    "net/url"
)
```

```
func main() {
  data := url.Values{}
  data.Set("s", "Golang")

  response, err := http.PostForm("https://hub.packtpub.com/", data)
  // ... Continue processing the response ...
}
```

In Go, you build a form submission using the `url.Values` struct. You can use this to set the inputs of the form—`s=Golang` in our case—and submit it using the `http.Post()` function. This technique will only help if the form uses POST as its method.

Avoiding loops

If you are building a web scraper that follows links, you might need to be aware of which pages you've already visited. It's quite possible that a page you are visiting contains a link to a page you have already visited, sending you into an infinite loop. Therefore, it is very important to build a tracking system into your scraper that records its history.

The simplest data structure for storing a unique collection of items would be a set. The Go standard library does not have a set data structure, but it can be emulated by using a `map[string]interface{}{}`.

 An `interface{}` in Go is a generic object, similar to `java.lang.Object`.

In Go, you can define a map as follows:

```
visitedMap := map[string]interface{}{}
```

In this case, we would use the visited URL as the key, and anything you want as the value. We will just use `nil`, because as long as the key is present, we know we have visited the site. Adding a site that we have visited would simply insert the URL as the key and `nil` as a value, as given in the following code block:

```
visitedMap["http://example.com/index.html"] = nil
```

When you try to retrieve a value from a map, using a given key, Go will return two values: the value for the key if it exists, and a Boolean, stating whether or not the key exists in the map. In our case, we are only concerned about the latter.

We would check for a site visit like the one demonstrated in the following code block:

```
_, ok := visitedMap["http://example.com/index.html"]

if ok {
  // ok == true, meaning the URL exists in the visitedMap
  // Skip this URL
} else {
  // ok == false, meaning the URL does not exist in the visitedMap
  // Make the HTTP Request and continue processing this page
  // ...
}
```

Breadth-first versus depth-first crawling

Now that you have the ability to navigate to different pages, as well as the ability to avoid getting stuck in a loop, you have one more important choice to make when crawling a website. In general, there are two main approaches to covering all pages by following links: breadth-first, and depth-first. Imagine that you are scraping a single web page that contains 20 links. Naturally, you would follow the first link on the page. On the second page, there are ten more links. Herein lies your decision: follow the first link on the second page, or go back to the second link on the first page.

Depth-first

If you choose to follow the first link on the second page, this would be considered depth-first crawling:

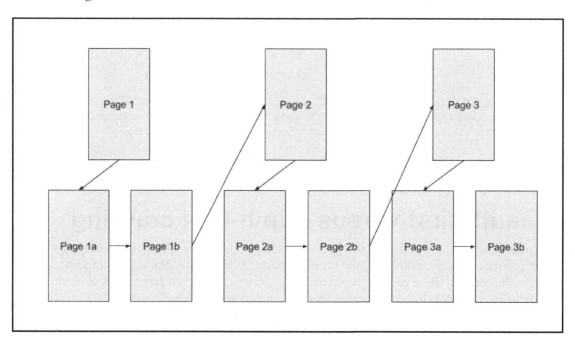

Your scraper will continue to follow the links as deeply as possible to collect all of the pages. In the case of products, you might be following a path of recommendations or similar items. This might take you to products far outside the original starting point of your scraper. On the other hand, it may also help build a tighter network of related items quickly. On websites containing articles, depth-first crawling will send you back in time quickly, as linked pages would most likely be a reference to a previously written article. This will help you reach the origins of many linked paths quickly.

In Chapter 6, *Protecting Your Web Scraper*, we will learn how to avoid some of the pitfalls of depth-first crawling by ensuring we have the proper boundaries in place.

Breadth-first

If you choose to follow the second link on the first page, this would be considered breadth-first crawling:

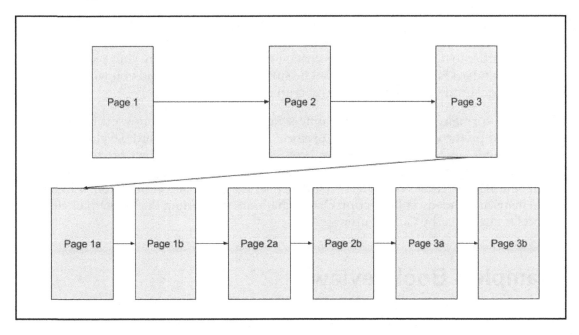

Using this technique, you would most likely stay within your original search domain for longer. For example, if you were on a website with products and initiated a search for shoes, the majority of the links on the page would be related to shoes. You would be collecting the links within the same domain first. As you move deeper within the website, recommended items may lead you to other types of clothing. Breadth-first crawling would help you collect full clusters of pages more quickly.

There is no right or wrong technique for how to navigate your scraper; it all depends on your specific needs. Depth-first crawling will reveal the origins of specific topics, whereas breadth-first crawling will complete a full cluster before discovering new content. You might even use a combination of techniques if this suits your requirements.

Navigating with JavaScript

So far we have focused on simple web pages where all of the information needed is only available in the HTML file. This is not always the case for more modern websites, which contain JavaScript code responsible for loading extra information after the initial page loads. In many websites, when you perform a search, the initial page might display with an empty table and, in the background, make a second request to collect the actual results to display. In order to do this, custom code written in JavaScript is run by your web browser. Using the standard HTTP client would not be sufficient in this case and you would need to use an external browser that supports JavaScript execution.

In Go, there are many options for integrating scraper code with web browsers thanks to a few standard protocols. The WebDriver protocol is the original standard developed by Selenium and is supported by most major browsers. This protocol allows programs to send a browser's commands, such as load a web page, wait for an element, click a button, and capture the HTML. These commands would be necessary to collect results from a web page where items are loaded via JavaScript. One such library supporting the WebDriver client protocol is `selenium` by GitHub user `tebeka`.

Example – Book reviews

On the Packt Publishing website, book reviews are loaded via JavaScript and are not visible when the page is first loaded. This example demonstrates how to use the `selenium` package to scrape reviews from a book listing on the Packt Publishing site.

The `selenium` package relies on four external dependencies in order to function properly:

- A Google Chrome or Mozilla Firefox web browser
- A WebDriver that is compatible with Chrome or Firefox, respectively
- The Selenium Server binary
- Java

All of these dependencies will be downloaded by the `selenium` script during installation, except for Java.

Please ensure that you have Java installed on your machine. If not, please download and install the official version from `https://www.java.com/en/download/help/download_options.xml`.

First, install the package via the following:

```
go get github.com/tebeka/selenium
```

This will install `selenium` inside your `GOPATH` at
`$GOPATH/src/github.com/tebeka/selenium`. This installation script relies on a number
of other packages in order to run. You can install them using the following commands:

```
go get cloud.google.com/go/storage
go get github.com/golang/glog
go get google.golang.org/api/option
```

Next, we install the browsers, drivers, and `selenium` binary that the code example needs.
Navigate to the `Vendor` folder inside the `selenium` directory and complete the installation
by running the following command:

```
go run init.go
```

Now that `selenium` and all of its dependencies are set up, you can create a new folder in
your `$GOPATH/src` with a `main.go` file. Let's step through the code that you will need to
write in order to collect reviews from a book. First, let's look at the `import` statement:

```
package main

import (
  "github.com/tebeka/selenium"
)
```

As you can see, our program only relies on the `selenium` package to run the example!
Next, we can see the beginning of the `main` function and define a few important variables:

```
func main() {

  // The paths to these binaries will be different on your machine!

  const (
    seleniumPath =
"/home/vincent/Documents/workspace/Go/src/github.com/tebeka/selenium/vendor
/selenium-server-standalone-3.14.0.jar"
    geckoDriverPath =
"/home/vincent/Documents/workspace/Go/src/github.com/tebeka/selenium/vendor
/geckodriver-v0.23.0-linux64"
  )
```

Here, we render the constants for the paths to the `selenium` server executable, and the path for the Firefox WebDriver, known as the `geckodriver`. If you were to run this example with Chrome, you would provide the path to your `chromedriver` instead. All of these files were installed by the `init.go` program run earlier and your paths will be different from the ones written here. Please be sure to change these to suit your environment. The next part of the function initializes the `selenium` driver:

```
service, err := selenium.NewSeleniumService(
  seleniumPath,
  8080,
  selenium.GeckoDriver(geckoDriverPath))

if err != nil {
  panic(err)
}
defer service.Stop()

caps := selenium.Capabilities{"browserName": "firefox"}
wd, err := selenium.NewRemote(caps, "http://localhost:8080/wd/hub")
if err != nil {
  panic(err)
}
defer wd.Quit()
```

`defer` statements tell Go to run the following command at the end of the function. It is good practice to defer your cleanup statements so you don't forget to put them at the end of your function!

Here, we create the `selenium` driver by providing the paths to the executable that it needs, as well as the port through which our code will communicate with the `selenium` server. We also obtain a connection to the WebDriver by calling `NewRemote()`. The `wd` object is the WebDriver connection that we will use to send commands to the Firefox browser, as demonstrated in the following code snippet:

```
err =
wd.Get("https://www.packtpub.com/networking-and-servers/mastering-go")
  if err != nil {
    panic(err)
  }

  var elems []selenium.WebElement
  wd.Wait(func(wd2 selenium.WebDriver) (bool, error) {
    elems, err = wd.FindElements(selenium.ByCSSSelector, "div.product-
reviews-review div.review-body")
    if err != nil {
```

```
        return false, err
    } else {
        return len(elems) > 0, nil
    }
})

for _, review := range elems {
    body, err := review.Text()
    if err != nil {
        panic(err)
    }
    println(body)
}
}
```

We tell the browser to load the web page for *Mastering Go*, by Mihalis Tsoukalos, and wait for our CSS query for product reviews to return more than one result. This will loop indefinitely until the reviews appear. Once we discover the reviews, we print the text for each one.

Summary

In this chapter, we covered the basics of how to navigate your web scraper through a website. We looked into the anatomy of a web link, and how to use HTTP GET requests to simulate following a link. We looked at how HTTP forms, such as search boxes, generate HTTP requests. We also saw the difference between HTTP GET and POST requests, and how to send POST requests in Go. We also covered how to avoid loops by tracking your history. Finally, the differences between breadth-first and depth-first web crawling, and their respective trade-offs were covered.

In Chapter 6, *Protecting Your Web Scraper*, we will look at ways to ensure your safety as you crawl the web.

6
Protecting Your Web Scraper

Now that you have built a web scraper that is capable of autonomously collecting information from various websites, there are a few things you should do to make sure it operates safely. A number of important measures should be taken to protect your web scraper. As you should be aware, nothing on the internet should be fully trusted if you do not have complete ownership of it.

In this chapter, we will discuss the following tools and techniques you will need to ensure your web scraper's safety:

- Virtual private servers
- Proxies
- Virtual private networks
- Whitelists and blacklists

Virtual private servers

When you make an HTTP request for a website, you are making a direct connection between your computer and the targeted server. By doing this, you are providing them with your machine's public IP address, which can be used to determine your general location, and your **Internet Service Provider** (**ISP**). Although this can't be tied directly back to your exact location, it could be used maliciously if its finds its way into the wrong hands. With this in mind, it is preferable to not expose any of your personal assets to untrusted servers.

Running your web scraper on a computer that is far removed from your physical location, with some sort of remote access, is a good way to decouple your web scraper from your personal computer. You can rent **Virtual Private Server** (**VPS**) instances from various providers on the web.

Some of the more notable companies include the following:

- **Amazon Web Services (AWS)**
- Microsoft Azure
- Google Cloud
- DigitalOcean
- Linode

These companies will allow you to create a virtual machine and provide you with credentials for accessing the instance. They have various offerings, depending on the size of machine you require, and most of them offer some free resources if they are below a certain size.

You will need to deploy your web scraping code onto these machines and run the program from within your VPS. This book will not cover the packaging and deployment of Go applications in detail, but the following are a few techniques for getting you started:

- **Secure Copy Protocol (SCP)**
- Git
- Ansible
- Puppet
- Docker
- Kubernetes

By operating the web scraper on a VPS, you will have the peace of mind that, should your machine become exposed, it can be safely destroyed without compromising your personal computer. Also, running your scraper in a VPS allows you to easily scale to suit your needs as you begin scraping more websites. You can spin up multiple VPS instances to run your scrapers in parallel.

Proxies

The role of a proxy is to provide an additional layer of protection on top of your system. At its core, a proxy is a server that sits in between your web scraper and the target web server, and passes communication between the two. Your web scraper sends a request to the proxy server, which then forwards the request to the website. From the point of view of the website, the request only comes from the proxy server, without any knowledge of the origin of the request. There are many types of proxy available, each with its own pros and cons

Public and shared proxies

Some proxies are open to the public to use. However, they can be shared by many different people. This jeopardizes your reliability because, if other users compromise the proxy through misuse, it could endanger your web scraper. Speed is another concern for public proxies: the more traffic flows through a proxy, the less bandwidth will be available. On the other hand, these proxies are free to use and could be useful during your testing and debugging stages.

A few sites listing public proxies are given as follows:

- `https://free-proxy-list.net`
- `https://hidemyna.me`
- `https://proxy-list.download`

With the varying success of public proxies that are available, you will need to ensure you do your research before trying them out in production. You will need to consider whether or not these proxies are reliable, and can reach your target website. You'll also need to ensure that your information is being protected as you connect through them.

Dedicated proxies

Dedicated proxies are a great way to ensure that only you are in control of the traffic flowing through the proxy servers. There are many companies that sell dedicated proxies both on-demand and in bulk. Some companies worth considering include the following:

- Storm proxies
- Blazing SEO
- Ghost proxies
- Oxylabs

There are a few things to consider when selecting a company.

Price

Pricing models for dedicated proxies vary from company to company. In most cases, you pay per IP address that you use and you will be able to use that IP address as much as you want. There are a number of companies that have a pool of IP addresses and will charge you based on your bandwidth instead. In this pricing model, you will need to ensure that you are making the most efficient calls possible.

The cost of a per-IP proxy can range between $1 and $6 per month. Usually, you will get larger discounts for buying in bulk. Some companies may also limit your bandwidth.

Location

On occasion, the location of the proxy may be important to you. Many proxy companies distribute their servers throughout the world to allow for greater coverage. If you are scraping websites in different countries, it might make sense for you to run your scraper through a proxy located in that country in order to avoid firewalls or unusual traffic signatures. Different countries also may have different laws about what is permissible through the internet in that country, so you should always consult local laws before pursuing this route

Type

There are two main types of proxy that you should be aware of: residential and data center proxies. Residential proxies have IP addresses that are assigned by an ISP that is registered in a residential area. The IP addresses are directly related to a specific region and many websites can estimate where you are based on these IP addresses. This is how Google Analytics knows where web traffic to your website is coming from. From a web scraping point of view, it may make a difference if the web traffic is coming from San Francisco as opposed to London. If your content changes based on your location, you may need residential proxies in the right places.

The second type of proxy is data center proxies. These proxies are assigned by ISPs that are related to data centers, such as VSP providers. When you create a new virtual machine, the IP address assigned to that machine is most likely a data center IP. These addresses may be intentionally blocked by websites to prevent access from non-residential visitors.

Anonymity

Anonymity should be considered quite high on the list when selecting proxy providers. Not all proxies completely hide the originating source of the request when they pass data to the target servers.

Transparent proxies provide the target server with information about who you are, and should be avoided in most cases. These proxies pass HTTP headers to the target server, such as `X-Forwarded-For: <your_ip_address>`, to identify the originating source of the request, and `Via: <proxy_server>` to identify the proxy itself.

Anonymous proxies provide the same headers as transparent proxies, but they may provide false information in order to hide your true identity. In this case, the target server will be aware that the connection is being made through a proxy, but the true source of the request is unknown.

Elite proxies are the highest level of anonymity that you can achieve from a proxy. Elite proxies do not forward any information about the originating source, nor do they disclose that the request is coming from a proxy. Instead, the request appears to the web server to be a normal request originating at the IP address of the proxy.

Proxies in Go

Once you've received a list of proxy addresses to use, configuring your Go HTTP client is very simple. The Go HTTP client contains an object called a **transport**. The transport is responsible for low-level communication with web servers, including opening and closing connections, sending and receiving data, and handling HTTP 1XX response codes. You can set the `Proxy()` method of transport by setting a function that accepts an `*http.Request`, and returns the proxy address as a `*url.URL`.

The following is an example of setting a `Proxy()` function:

```
package main

import (
    "math/rand"
    "net/http"
    "net/url"
)

// Public proxies from https://hidemyna.me
// These proxies are subject to frequent change.
// Please replace them if necessary.
```

```go
var proxies []string = []string{
 "http://207.154.231.208:8080",
 "http://138.68.230.88:8080",
 "http://162.243.107.45:8080",
}

func GetProxy(_ *http.Request) (*url.URL, error) {
  randomIndex := rand.Int31n(int32(len(proxies)) - int32(1))
  randomProxy := proxies[randomIndex]
  return url.Parse(randomProxy)
}

func main() {
  http.DefaultTransport.(*http.Transport).Proxy = GetProxy
  // Continue with your HTTP requests ...
}
```

The `GetProxy()` function randomly chooses between the three configured proxies and converts the string to a `*url.URL`. By configuring the `http.DefaultTransport.Proxy` function, each time the `http.DefaultClient` is used, `GetProxy` will determine which random proxy to use. You could also use different proxies for different hosts, by inspecting the `*http.Request` and returning your desired proxy based on the hostname provided.

Virtual private networks

Depending on your need, you may need to connect to a **Virtual Private Network (VPN)** in order to ensure that all of your web scraping traffic is hidden. Where proxies provide a layer of protection by masking the IP address of your web scraper, a VPN also masks the data that flows between your scraper and the target site through an encrypted tunnel. This will make the content that you are scraping invisible to ISPs and anyone else with access to your network.

 VPNs are not legal in all countries. Please comply with local laws.

There are many companies that offer VPN access, with costs typically ranging from $5 to $15 per month.

Some recommended companies are listed as follows:

- Vypr VPN
- Express VPN
- IPVanish VPN
- Nord VPN

Configuring your web scraper to use the VPN is different from proxies. VPNs usually require a specific client to connect your machine to their network, which is not done through code. The advantage is that the code you write with your scraper will work independently of any network configuration. Unfortunately, you will not be able to incorporate on-the-fly changes in your network in code without using shell commands.

Follow the instructions supplied by your VPN provider in order to connect to a VPN network.

Boundaries

When you are crawling a website, you may not always know where you will end up. Many links in web pages take you to external sites that you may not trust as much as your target sites. These linked pages could contain irrelevant information or could be used for malicious purposes. It is important to define boundaries for your web scraper to safely navigate through unknown sources.

Whitelists

Whitelisting domains is a process by means of which you explicitly allow your scraper to access certain websites. Any site listed on the whitelist is OK for the web scraper to access, whereas any site that is not listed is automatically skipped. This is a simple way to ensure that your scraper only accesses pages for a small set of specific sites, which helps in the collection of very focused information. You can take this even further by only allowing access to paths of a website.

Building a whitelist in Go is fairly simple with the use of the URL and path packages. Let's take an example of indexing articles on the Packt Hub site (`https://hub.packtpub.com/`). Many of the articles posted here contain links to external websites for the purpose of noting their sources of information. However, if we are only interested in finding other articles on Packt Hub, we would whitelist only `hub.packtpub.com` URLs.

An example article link you may encounter would look something like this: `https://hub.packtpub.com/8-programming-languages-to-learn-in-2019/`.

Using the GoLang URL package, we can look at the hostname to determine whether it is a link worth following:

```
parsedUrl, err :=
url.Parse("https://hub.packtpub.com/8-programming-languages-to-learn-in-201
9")

if err != nil {
  panic(err)
}

site := parsedUrl.Host + parsedUrl.Path
```

You could then verify that this matches by using the `path.Match()` function, shown as follows:

```
doesMatch, err := path.Match("hub.packtpub.com/*", site)
if err != nil {
  panic(err)
}
if doesMatch {
// Continue scraping ...
}
```

Blacklists

Contrary to whitelists, **blacklists** define websites where your scraper should definitely not venture. Sites that you will want to include here may be places that you know do not contain any relevant information, or you are just not interested in their content. You might also temporarily blacklist sites that are experiencing performance issues, such as a high number of 5XX errors, as discussed in `Chapter 2`, *The Request/Response Cycle*. You can match your link URLs to their hostname in the same way as in the preceding example.

The only change that is required is to modify the last `if` block, shown as follows, so it runs only if `doesMatch` is false:

```
if !doesMatch {
// Continue scraping ...
}
```

Summary

In this chapter, we reviewed a number of different techniques to ensure that we and our web scrapers are protected while browsing the internet. By using VPS, we are protecting our personal assets from malicious activity and discoverability on the internet. Proxies also help restrict information about the source of internet traffic, providing a layer of anonymity. VPNs add an extra layer of security over proxies by creating an encrypted tunnel for our data to flow through. Finally, creating whitelists and blacklists ensures that your scraper will not venture too deep into uncharted and undesirable places.

In Chapter 7, *Scraping with Concurrency*, we will look at how to use concurrency in order to increase the scale of our web scraper without the added cost of incorporating extra resources.

7
Scraping with Concurrency

As you begin to add more and more target websites into your scraping requirements, you will eventually hit a point where you wish you could make more calls, faster. In a single program, the crawl delay might add extra time to your scraper, adding unnecessary time to process the other sites. Do you see the problem in the following diagram?

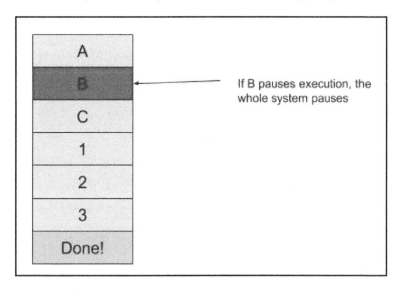

If these two sites could be run in parallel, there would not be any interference. Maybe the time to access and parse a page is longer than the crawl delay for this website, and launching a second request before the processing of the first response completes could save you time as well. Look how the situation is improved in the following diagram:

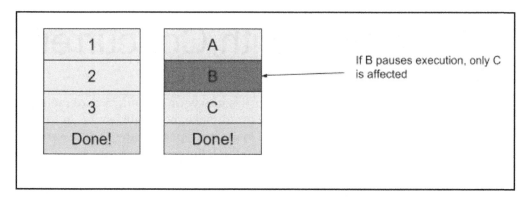

In any of these cases, you will need to introduce concurrency into your web scraper.

In this chapter, we will cover the following topics:

- What is concurrency
- Concurrency pitfalls
- Go concurrency model
- sync package helpers

What is concurrency

Instructions in a program are run by a **central processing unit (CPU)**. This CPU can run multiple threads, which can process instructions for separate tasks, together. This is achieved by switching between the two tasks and executing the instructions in an alternating fashion, like pulling together two sides of a zipper. This overlapping execution of tasks is called concurrency. For the sake of simplicity, we will describe it as performing multiple tasks at the same time. The following diagram shows how it may appear:

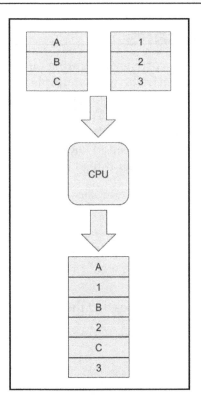

Concurrency should not be confused with parallelism, where two things or instructions can literally be executed at the same time.

By introducing a concurrent architecture to your web scraper, you will be able to make multiple web requests to different sites without waiting for one site to respond. In this way, a slow site or bad connection to one server will only affect the task of scraping that specific site and not the others. As the majority of the time spent in web scraping is communication over a network, this is a very good solution to your problem.

Building a program with a concurrent architecture can sometimes be a daunting task, as it opens up a new set of issues that need to be taken into consideration. When multiple threads are running, they will typically need some mechanism for communication and must be very careful about trying to modify the same objects at the same time. Without a well-thought-out approach, your scraper is bound to encounter a variety of problems that can be very difficult to detect and fix.

Concurrency pitfalls

The source of most issues with concurrency is figuring out how to share information safely, and provide access to that information, between multiple threads. The simplest solution would seem to be to have an object that both threads can have access to, and modify, in order to communicate with the other thread. This seemingly innocent strategy is easier suggested than done. Let's look at this example, where two threads are sharing the same stack of web pages to scrape. They will need to know which web pages have been completed, and which web pages the other thread is currently working on.

We will use a simple map for this example, as shown in the following code:

```
siteStatus := map[string]string{
  "http://example.com/page1.html" : "READY",
  "http://example.com/page2.html" : "READY",
  "http://example.com/page3.html" : "READY",
}
```

 The "READY" status indicates that the site has not yet been scraped.

Race conditions

From the start, this strategy has a major issue. If both threads look at the map at the same time, they will see that page1.html is ready to be scraped. They would then both update the value for page1.html to "WORKING", and go on to scrape the same site at the same time! This would not only be a duplicated effort, but it would also create an extra load on the example.com server. An even worse situation is if one thread is updating the status to "WORKING" while the other thread is attempting to read the status. Then, your scraper will crash. Concurrent read and/or write operations are not allowed in Go.

This situation is known as a race condition and is one of the most common issues you will run into as you build concurrent programs. In order to prevent race conditions from happening, there needs to be a mechanism where one thread can block access to the map for all other threads. The Go standard library provides the sync package to hold many helpful tools for building concurrent applications. In our specific situation, a sync.Mutex would be a very helpful tool.

You can also use the "-race" flag with many of the Go commands (such as: go run and go test) to help detect race conditions and provide helpful information. See more in their blog post at https://blog.golang.org/race-detector.

The sync.Mutex is a lockable object that acts as a barrier for other objects, much like the lock on a door. In order to enter the room, you first check if the door is locked. If it is locked, you must wait for someone to unlock it before you can proceed. The following code is a sample of how you would use a sync.Mutex in Go to protect concurrent reads and writes to our map:

```
mtx := *sync.Mutex{}

mtx.Lock()
if siteStatus["http://example.com/page1.html"] == "READY" {
  siteStatus["http://example.com/page1.html"] = "WORKING"
}
mtx.Unlock()
```

When a thread calls mtx.Lock(), it first checks if there is an existing lock being held by any other thread. If there is already an existing lock being held, your thread will wait until the existing lock is released. Only one thread can hold a lock at any given time, just like the door mentioned before.

When access to an object allows for concurrent reads, but must protect the object when a write is in process, the sync package provides the sync.RWMutex struct. This works similarly to the sync.Mutex, except that it separates locking into two separate methods:

- Lock() / Unlock(): A lock used specifically when a write operation is in progress
- RLock() / RUnlock(): A lock used specifically when a read operation is in progress

Multiple threads can obtain read locks without blocking access to the object, except for threads attempting to obtain a write lock. Along the same lines, a read lock cannot be obtained if the write lock exists. Using the RWMutex, the preceding example would look like the following one:

```
mtx := *sync.RWMutex{}

mtx.RLock()
if siteStatus["http://example.com/page1.html"] == "READY" {
  mtx.RUnlock()
  mtx.Lock()
```

```
    siteStatus["http://example.com/page1.html"] = "WORKING"
    mtx.UnLock()
} else{
    mtx.RUnlock()
}
```

The thread obtains a read lock before checking the map, to ensure that no writes are being made. Then it releases the read lock, regardless of whether the `if` a statement is `true` or `false`, and obtains a write lock before updating the map. Using these two type of mutexes will help protect your scraper from race conditions. However, it can also add another common concurrency pitfall.

Deadlocks

When adding locks and unlocking code to a concurrent application, at some point you may see that your application has completely stopped, but not crashed. After much time spent digging through the code, adding extra print statements, and stepping through a debugger, you finally see it; a lock was not released! This situation is what is known as a deadlock.

The Go standard library does not have any tools to help detect and overcome deadlocks. However, there is support in the open source community. One such package being `go-deadlock` by GitHub user `sacha-s`. The `go-deadlock` package provides a drop-in replacement for the `sync.Mutex` and the `sync.RWMutex`, that monitors how long a lock on an object has been held. By default, when it detects a deadlock, it will exit the program.

The deadlock timeout duration and the action to take are both configurable through the `deadlock.Opts` object, as shown in the following example:

```
deadlock.Opts.DeadlockTimeout = 120 * time.Second // 2 minute timeout
deadlock.Opts.OnPotentialDeadlock = func() {
    printf("Deadlock detected")
    beginGracefulShutdown()  // This is a hypothetical function
}
```

Using mutexes and deadlock detections are some of the standard ways of ensuring that concurrent threads can operate without getting in each other's way. These traditional methods are offered through the Go programming language. However, they provide a different perspective on how concurrent threads should communicate with one another.

The Go concurrency model

As you have seen, many of the problems with concurrent programs stem from sharing memory resources between multiple threads. This shared memory is used to communicate state and can be very fragile, with great care needed to ensure that everything stays up and running. In Go, concurrency is approached with the mantra:

Do not communicate by sharing memory; instead, share memory by communicating.

When you use mutexes and locks around a common object, you are communicating by sharing memory. Multiple threads look to the same memory location to alert and to provide information for the other threads to use. Instead of doing this, Go provides tools to help share memory by communicating.

Goroutines

Up until this point, we have been referring to concurrent paths of execution as threads. In Go, the synonymous tool for accomplishing this is called a **goroutine**. Goroutines are described as a:

Lightweight thread of execution.

Unlike traditional threads found in C and Java, goroutines are managed by the Go runtime and not the OS thread scheduler. This allows the Go runtime scheduler to be hyper-focused on only tasks in the Go program. It also leverages OS threads as needed, providing more granular units of operation. OS threads suffer from a large amount of overhead required to create each thread and a relatively slow ability to determine which thread a task should be run on. The Go runtime chooses much smaller footprints when creating separations of goroutines, allowing more of them to run simultaneously.

Creating goroutines is, by design, a very simple task in Go. By prefixing any function call with the word `go`, it will run the function in a new goroutine. The following example is a simple program that runs a small goroutine:

```
package main

import (
  "fmt"
  "time"
)

func startTicker() {
  ticks := 0
```

```
for true {
fmt.Println(ticks)
ticks++
time.Sleep(1 * time.Second)
}
}

func main() {
println("Starting ticker")
go startTicker()
time.Sleep(10 * time.Second)
}
```

When you run this code, you can see that the numbers from `startTicker()` are printed, even though the main goroutine sleeps for 10 seconds. If you modify this code, changing the Go `startTicker()` with just `startTicker()`, this code will run forever, printing each second until the process is killed forcefully.

When multiple goroutines need to communicate with each other, Go provides a simple tool for them to use.

Channels

Channels are conduits through which goroutines can send and receive information. This sits at the core of the Go's concurrency model for sharing memory through communicating. Channels allow for goroutines to each other rather than trying to access the same information. Channels are also unidirectional, meaning that data can only flow in one direction, as shown in the following diagram:

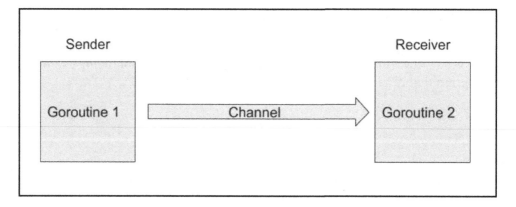

If communication is needed in both directions, two channels will need to be used.

In our previous example using mutexes, multiple threads attempted to access the map containing the status of each website by creating a release lock. We can use channels as a safer approach by launching the scraper threads as separate goroutines and having them communicate their status back to the main goroutine through a channel. This is shown in the following example:

```go
package main

func scrapeSite(url string, statusChan chan map[string]string) {
  // Performing scraping operations...
  statusChan <- map[string]string{url: "DONE"}
}

func main() {
  siteStatus := map[string]string{
    "http://example.com/page1.html": "READY",
    "http://example.com/page2.html": "READY",
    "http://example.com/page3.html": "READY",
  }

  updatesChan := make(chan map[string]string)

  numberCompleted := 0
  for site := range siteStatus {
    siteStatus[site] = "WORKING"
    go scrapeSite(site, updatesChan)
  }

  for update := range updatesChan {
    for url, status := range update {
      siteStatus[url] = status
      numberCompleted++
    }
    if numberCompleted == len(siteStatus) {
      close(updatesChan)
    }
  }
}
```

In the main function for this program, the updatesChan is created to act as the means through which goroutines can provide their status back to the main goroutine. These goroutines are started in the first for loop by calling Go scrapeSite, which takes the URL of the website to be scraped, and a reference to the updatesChan. The main goroutine then enters a second for loop where it listens for data to come through updatesChan, providing a new status update for any of the URLs. As each site provides an update, the number of completed sites is incremented until all of the sites have completed. At this point, the main goroutine closes the channel.

 Closing a channel prevents the sending and receiving of any more data through that channel. As far as for-range operations are concerned, this marks the end of the stream, exiting to loop.

By converting the method of communication to use channels, there is only one owner of the shared data and the responsibility of updating the map falls back on a single goroutine. This allows each worker of goroutine to provide status updates safely, without the need for locks, or sharing memory.

sync package helpers

Goroutines and channels, being the core constructs of concurrent programming in Go, will provide most of the utility that you will need. However, there are many helpful objects that the Go standard library provides that are also useful to know. We have already seen how sync.Mutex and sync.RWMutex work, but let's take a look at some of the other objects offered.

Conditions

Now that you are able to launch scraper tasks into multiple threads, some controls will need to be put into place so things don't get too out of hand. It is very simple in Go to launch 1,000 goroutines to scrape 1,000 pages simultaneously from a single program. However, your machine most likely cannot handle the same load. The sync package provides a few utilities to help maintain order in your web scraper.

One common control that you will want to put into place is the number of active concurrent scraping threads. Before you launch a new goroutine, you will need to satisfy a certain condition, being that the number of active threads is less than some value. If this condition fails the check, your new goroutine will have to wait, until it is signaled that the condition passes. This scenario is solved using the `sync.Cond` object.

The `sync.Cond` object provides a mechanism to tell goroutines to wait until a signal is received, based on any defined condition. A `sync.Cond` struct wraps a `sync.Locker` (usually a `sync.Mutex` or `sync.RWMutex`) to control access to the condition itself. There follows an example of how you might use a `sync.Cond` to control the number of active scraper threads:

```
package main

import (
  "sync"
  "time"
)

var sites []string = []string{
  "http://example.com/site1.html",
  "http://example.com/site2.html",
  "http://example.com/site3.html",
}
var activeThreads = 0
var doneCount = 0
const maxActiveThreads = 1

func scrapeSite(site string, condition *sync.Cond) {
  condition.L.Lock()
  if activeThreads >= maxActiveThreads {
    condition.Wait()
  }
  activeThreads++
  condition.L.Unlock()
  println("scraping " + site)
  // Scraping code goes here ...
  condition.L.Lock()

  activeThreads--
  doneCount++
  condition.L.Unlock()
  condition.Signal()
}

func main() {
```

```
    var l = sync.Mutex{}
    var c = sync.NewCond(&l)

    for _, site := range sites {
      println("starting scraper for " + site)
      go scrapeSite(site, c)
    }
    for doneCount < len(sites){
      time.Sleep(1 * time.Second)
    }
    println("Done!")
}
```

The main focus of this code is inside the `scrapeSite()` function. In this part of the code, the program first checks if it has reached the maximum number of concurrent threads. If this condition is true, it will wait. This pauses the goroutine until a `Signal()` or a `Broadcast()` is called from the `sync.Cond`. We use `Signal()` in our case to notify a single goroutine that the condition has passed, and that it can proceed. If `Broadcast()` was used here, it would release all of the goroutines which are currently waiting on the condition. A good use case for that could be pausing the entire system to make some configuration change on the `fly`, then resuming all paused goroutines.

Atomic counters

In the previous example, we surrounded any increment or decrement of `activeThreads` with a `Lock()` / `Unlock()`. This can become quite verbose if it needs to be done multiple times, as in our case. The `sync` package offers a subpackage called atomic that provides methods for updating objects without the need for locks. This is done by creating a new variable each time a change is made, while preventing multiple writes from occurring at the same time. The following example shows some of the changes necessary to use `activeThreads` as an `atomic` counter:

```
package main

import (
  "sync"
  "sync/atomic"
)
// ...
var activeThreads int32 = 0
// ...
func scrapeSite(site string, condition *sync.Cond) {
  condition.L.Lock()
  if activeThreads >= maxActiveThreads {
```

```
condition.Wait()
}
condition.L.Unlock()

atomic.AddInt32(&activeThreads, 1)
// Scraping code goes here ...
atomic.AddInt32(&activeThreads, -1)
condition.Signal()
}
// ...
```

Summary

In this chapter, we discussed many topics surrounding concurrency in web scraping. We looked at what concurrency is and how we can benefit from it. We reviewed some of the common issues that must be avoided when building concurrent programs. We also learned about the Go concurrency model and how to use its primitive objects to build concurrent Go applications. Finally, we looked at a few of the niceties Go has included in its `sync` package. In our final chapter, we will look at taking our scraper to the highest level.

8
Scraping at 100x

By now, you should have a very broad understanding of how to build a solid web scraper. Up to this point, you have learned how to collect information from the internet efficiently, safely, and respectfully. The tools that you have at your disposal are enough to build web scrapers on a small to medium scale, which may be just what you need to accomplish your goals. However, there may come a day when you need to upscale your application to handle large and production-sized projects. You may be lucky enough to make a living out of offering services, and, as that business grows, you will need an architecture that is robust and manageable. In this chapter, we will review the architectural components that make a good web scraping system, and look at example projects from the open source community. Here are the topics we will discuss:

- Components of a web scraping system
- Scraping HTML pages with colly
- Scraping JavaScript pages with chrome-protocol
- Distributed scraping with dataflowkit

Components of a web scraping system

In Chapter 7, *Scraping with Concurrency*, about concurrency, we saw how defining a clear separation of roles between the worker goroutines and the main goroutine helped mitigate issues in the program. By clearly giving the main goroutine the responsibility of maintaining the state of the target URLs, and allowing the scraper threads to focus on scraping, we laid the groundwork for making a modular system which can easily scale components independently. This separation of concerns is the foundation for building large-scale systems of any kind.

There are a few main components that make up a web scraper. Each of these components should be able to scale without affecting other parts of the system, if they are properly decoupled. You will know if this decoupling is solid if you can break this system into its own package and reuse it for other projects. You might even want to release it to the open source community! Let's take a look at some of these components.

Queue

Before a web scraper can start collecting information, it needs to know where to go. It also needs to know where it has been. A proper queuing system will accomplish both of these goals. Queues can be set up in many different ways. In many of the previous examples, we used a `[]string` or a `map[string]string` to hold the target URLs the scraper should pursue. This works for smaller scale web scrapers where the work is being pushed to the workers.

In larger applications, a work-stealing queue would be preferred. In a work-stealing queue, the worker threads would take the first available job out of the queue as fast as they can accomplish the task. This way, if you need your system to increase throughput, you can simply add more worker threads. In this system, the queue does not need to concern itself with the status of the workers, and focuses only on the status of the jobs. This is beneficial to systems that push to the workers because it must be aware of how many workers there are, which workers are busy or free, and handles workers coming on and offline.

Queuing systems are not always a part of the main scraping application. There are many suitable solutions for external queues, such as databases, or streaming platforms, such as Redis and Kafka. These tools will support your queuing system to the limits of your own imagination.

Cache

As we have seen in `Chapter 3`, *Web Scraping Etiquette*, caching web pages is an essential part of an efficient web scraper. With a cache, we are able to avoid requesting content from a website if we know nothing has changed. In our previous examples, we used a local cache which saves the content into a folder on the local machine. In larger web scrapers with multiple machines, this causes problems, as each machine would need to maintain its own cache. Having a shared caching solution would solve this problem and increase the efficiency of your web scraper.

There are many different ways to approach this problem. Much like the queuing system, a database can help store a cache of your information. Most databases support storage of binary objects, so whether you are storing HTML pages, images, or any other content, it is possible to put it into a database. You can also include a lot of metadata about a file, such as a date it was recovered, the date it expires, the size, the Etag, and so on. Another caching solution you can use is a form of cloud object storage, such as Amazon S3, Google Cloud Store, and Microsoft object storage. These services typically offer low-cost storage solutions that mimic a file system and require a specific SDK, or use of their APIs. A third solution you could use is a **Network File System** (**NFS**) where each node would connect. Writing to cache on an NFS would be the same as if it were on the local file system, as far as your scraper code is concerned. There can be challenges in configuring your worker machines to connect to an NFS. Each of these approaches has its own unique set of pros and cons, depending on your own setup.

Storage

In most cases, when you are scraping the web, you will be looking for very specific information. This is probably going to be a very small amount of data relative to the size of the web page itself. Because of the cache stores the entire contents of the web page, you will need some other storage system to store the parsed information. The storage component of a web scraper could be as simple as a text file, or as large as a distributed database.

These days, there are many database solutions available to satisfy different needs. If you have data that has many intricate relationships, then an SQL database might be a good fit for you. If you have data that has more of a nested structure, then you may want to look at NoSQL databases. There are also solutions that offer full-text indexing to make searching for documents easier, and time-series databases if you need to relate your data to some chronological order. Because there is no one-size-fits-all solution, the Go standard library only offers a package to handle the most common family of databases through the sql package.

The sql package was built to provide a common set of functions used to communicate with SQL databases such as MySQL, PostgreSQL, and Couchbase. For each of these databases, a separate driver has been written to fit into the framework defined by the sql package. These drivers, along with various others, can be found on GitHub and easily integrated with your project. The core of the sql package provides methods for opening and closing database connections, querying the database, iterating through rows of results, and performing inserts and modifications to the data. By mandating a standard interface for drivers, Go allows you to swap out your database for another SQL database with less effort.

Logs

One system that is often overlooked during the design of a scraping system is the logging system. It is important, first and foremost, to have clear log statements without logging too many unnecessary items. These statements should be informing the operator of the current status of scraping and any errors, or successes, the scraper encounters. This helps you get a picture of the overall health of your web scraper.

The simplest logging that can be done is printing messages to the terminal with `println()` or `fmt.Println()` type statements. This works well enough for a single node, but, as your scraper grows into a distributed architecture, it causes problems. In order to check how things are running in your system an operator would need to log into each machine to look at the logs. If there is an actual problem in the system, it may be difficult to diagnose by trying to piece together logs from multiple sources. A logging system built for distributed computing would be ideal at this point.

There are many logging solutions available in the open source world. One of the more popular choices is Graylog. Setting up a Graylog server is a simple process, requiring a MongoDB database and an Elasticsearch database to support it. Graylog defines a JSON format called GELF for sending log data to its servers, and accepts a very flexible set of keys. Graylog servers can accept log streams from multiple sources and you can define post-processing actions as well, such as reformatting data and sending alerts based on user-defined rules. There are many other similar systems, as well as paid services, that offer very similar features.

As there are various logging solutions, the open source community has built a library that eases the burden of integrating with different systems. The `logrus` package by GitHub user `sirupsen` provides a standard utility for writing log statements, as well as a plugin architecture for log formatters. Many people have built formatters for logging statements, including one for GELF statements to be sent to a Graylog server. If you decide to change your logging server during the development of your scraper, you need only to change the formatter instead of replacing all of your log statements.

Scraping HTML pages with colly

`colly` is one of the available projects on GitHub that covers most of the systems discussed earlier. This project is built to run on a single machine, due to its reliance on a local cache and queuing system.

The main worker object in `colly`, the `Collector`, is built to run in its own goroutine, allowing you to run multiple `Collectors` simultaneously. This design offers you the ability to scrape from multiple sites at the same time with different parameters, such as crawl delays, white and blacklists, and proxies.

`colly` is built to only process HTML and XML files. It does not offer support for JavaScript execution. However, you would be surprised at how much information you can collect with pure HTML. The following example is adapted from the GitHub README:

```go
package main

import (
  "github.com/gocolly/colly"
  "fmt"
)

func main() {
  c := colly.NewCollector(colly.AllowedDomains("go-colly.org"))

  // Find and visit all links
  c.OnHTML("a[href]", func(e *colly.HTMLElement) {
    e.Request.Visit(e.Attr("href"))
  })

  c.OnRequest(func(r *colly.Request) {
    fmt.Println("Visiting", r.URL)
  })

  c.Visit("http://go-colly.org/")
}
```

Before running this example, download `colly` via:
`go get github.com/gocolly/colly/...`

In this example, a `Collector` is created and defines a whitelist for `go-colly.org`, and a callback using the `OnHTML()` function. In this function, it performs a CSS query for `<a>` tags containing the `href` attribute. The callback specifies that the collector should navigate to the endpoint contained in that link. For each new page it visits, it repeats the process of visiting each link. Another callback is added to the collector using the `OnRequest()` function. This callback prints the name of the URL of each site it visits. As you can see, the `Collector` performs a depth-first crawl of the website because it follows each link as deep as it can go, before checking the other links on the same page.

`colly` provides many other features, such as respecting `robots.txt`, an extendable storage system for the queue, and various callbacks for different events in the system. This project is a great starting point for any web scraper that only requires HTML pages. It does not need much to set up and have a flexible system for parsing HTML pages.

Scraping JavaScript pages with chrome-protocol

In `Chapter 5`, *Web Scraping Navigation*, we looked at navigating websites that require JavaScript using `selenium` and the WebDriver protocol. There is another protocol that has been developed recently that offers many more features you can take advantage of to drive a web browser. The Chrome DevTools Protocol was started for use on Chrome browsers, but it has been adopted by the *W3C's Web Platform Incubator Community Group* as a project. The major web browsers work together to develop a standard protocol called the DevTools Protocol to adopt for all of their browsers.

The DevTools Protocol allows external programs to connect to a web browser and send commands to run JavaScript, and collect information from the browser. Most importantly, the protocol allows the program to collect the HTML on demand. This way, if you were scraping a web page in which search results were loaded via JavaScript, you could wait for the results to display, request the HTML page, and continue parsing the information needed.

The `chrome-protocol` project on GitHub, developed by the GitHub user `4ydx`, provides access to use the DevTools Protocol to drive compatible web browsers. Because these browsers expose a port, much like a web server does, you can run browsers on multiple machines. Using the `chrome-protocol` package, you would connect to the browser through a port and start building a series of tasks such as:

- `Navigate`: Opens a web page
- `FindAll`: Searches for elements by CSS query
- `Click`: Sends click events to a specific element

There are many more actions that you can send to a browser, and, by building your own custom script, you can navigate through JavaScript websites and collect the data that you need.

Example – Amazon Daily Deals

In the following example, we will use `chrome-protocol` and `goquery` to retrieve the Daily Deals from `amazon.com`. This example is a bit complex so the program has been broken into smaller chunks, which we will go through piece by piece. Let's begin with the package and `import` statements, as shown in the following code:

```
package main

import (
  "encoding/json"
  "fmt"
  "strings"
  "time"

  "github.com/4ydx/cdp/protocol/dom"
  "github.com/4ydx/chrome-protocol"
  "github.com/4ydx/chrome-protocol/actions"
  "github.com/PuerkitoBio/goquery"
)
```

This block of code imports the necessary packages to run the rest of the program. Some new packages that we have not seen before are:

- `encoding/json`: Go standard library for handling JSON data
- `github.com/4ydx/chrome-protocol`: Open source library for using the DevTools Protocol
- `github.com/4ydx/chrome-protocol/actions`: Open source library defining the DevTools Protocol actions
- `github.com/4ydx/cdp/protocol/dom`: Open source library for handling DOM nodes with `chrome-protocol`

The rest of the imported libraries should be familiar to you as we have used them in previous chapters. Next, we will define two functions: one function for retrieving the HTML page from Amazon, and the second to parse the results with `goquery`. The following code shows the function for retrieving the HTML data:

```
func getHTML() string {
  browser := cdp.NewBrowser("/usr/bin/google-chrome", 9222, "browser.log")
  handle := cdp.Start(browser, cdp.LogBasic)
  err := actions.EnableAll(handle, 2*time.Second)
  if err != nil {
    panic(err)
  }
  _, err = actions.Navigate(handle, "https://www.amazon.com/gp/goldbox",
    30*time.Second)
  if err != nil {
    panic(err) }

  var nodes []dom.Node
  retries := 5

  for len(nodes) == 0 && retries > 0 {
    nodes, err = actions.FindAll(
      handle,
      "div.GB-M-COMMON.GB-SUPPLE:first-child #widgetContent",
      10*time.Second)
    retries--
    time.Sleep(1 * time.Second)
  }

  if len(nodes) == 0 || retries == 0 {
    panic("could not find results")
  }

  reply, err := actions.Evaluate(handle, "document.body.outerHTML;",
30*time.Second)
  if err != nil {
    panic(err)
  }

  a := struct{
    Value string
  }{}
  json.Unmarshal([]byte("{\"value\":" + string(*reply.Result.Value)+"}"),
&a)
  body := a.Value

  handle.Stop(false)
```

```
    browser.Stop()
    return body
}
```

The function begins by opening a new instance of a Google Chrome browser and obtaining a handle for it for future commands. We use the `actions.EnableAll()` function to ensure that all of the events happening in the Chrome browser are sent back to our program so we do not miss anything. Next, we navigate to `https://www.amazon.com/gp/goldbox`, which is Amazon's Daily Deals web page.

 If you were to retrieve this page with a simple `GET` command, you would get a fairly empty shell of HTML code with a lot of JavaScript files waiting to be run. Making the request in the browser automatically runs the JavaScript that populates the remaining content.

The function then enters a `for` loop which checks for our HTML element that contains the daily deals data to populate in the page. The `for` loop will check every second for 5 seconds (as defined by the retries variable) before it either finds results or gives up. If there are no results, we exit the program. Next, the function sends a request to the browser to retrieve the `<body>` element via a JavaScript command. The processing of the results is a bit tricky as the value of the reply needs to be processed as a JSON string in order to return the raw HTML content. Once the content is parsed out, the function returns it.

The second function, responsible for parsing the HTML content is as follows:

```
func parseProducts(htmlBody string) []string {
    rdr := strings.NewReader(htmlBody)
    body, err := goquery.NewDocumentFromReader(rdr)
    if err != nil {
        panic(err)
    }

    products := []string{}
    details := body.Find("div.dealDetailContainer")
    details.Each(func(_ int, detail *goquery.Selection) {
        println(".")
        title := detail.Find("a#dealTitle").Text()
        price := detail.Find("div.priceBlock").Text()

        title = strings.TrimSpace(title)
        price = strings.TrimSpace(price)

        products = append(products, title + "\n"+price)
    })
    return products
}
```

Much like the example, we saw in Chapter 4, *Parsing HTML*, we use goquery to first look for the HTML element that contains the results. Within that container, we iterate through the details for each daily deal item, pulling out the title and the price for each item. We then append each product's title and price string to an array and return that array.

The main function ties these two functions together, first retrieving the body of the HTML page, then passing that on to parse the results. The main function then prints the title and price of each of the daily deals. The main function is as follows:

```
func main() {
  println("getting HTML...")
  html := getHTML()
  println("parsing HTML...")
  products := parseProducts(html)

  println("Results:")
  for _, product := range products {
    fmt.Println(product + "\n")
  }
}
```

As you can see, driving a web browser can be more difficult than scraping with just simple HTTP requests, but it can be done.

Distributed scraping with dataflowkit

Now that you have seen the progression of building fully featured web scrapers, I would like to introduce you to the most complete web scraping project in Go that has been built today. dataflowkit, by GitHub user slotix, is a fully featured web scraper that is modular and extensible for building scalable, large-scale distributed applications. It allows for multiple backends for storage of cached and computed information and is capable of both simple HTTP requests as well as driving browsers through the DevTools Protocol. Going above and beyond, dataflowkit has both a command-line interface and a JSON format to declare web scraping scripts.

The architecture of `dataflowkit` is separated into two distinct parts: fetching and parsing. Both Fetch and Parse phases of the system are built as separate binaries to be run on different machines. They communicate over HTTP via an API, as would you if you need to send or receive any information. By running these as separate entities, fetching operations and parsing operations can scale independently as the system grows. Depending on what type of sites you scrape, you may need more fetchers than scrapers, as JavaScript sites tend to require more resources. Once the page has been received, parsing the page often provides little overhead.

To get started using `dataflowkit`, you can either clone it from GitHub using the following code:

```
git clone https://github.com/slotix/dataflowkit
```

or via `go get`, using the following code:

```
go get github.com/slotix/dataflowkit/...
```

The Fetch service

The Fetch service is responsible for retrieving HTML data either via simple HTTP requests, or driving a web browser such as Google Chrome. To get started using the Fetch service, first, navigate to your local repository and run `go build` from the `cmd/fetch.d` directory. Once the build completes, you can start the service via `./fetch.d`.

 An instance of Google Chrome browser must be started prior to starting the Fetch service. This instance must be started with the `--remote-debugging-port` option set (usually to 9222). You may use the `--headless` flag as well to run without displaying any content.

The Fetch service is now ready to accept commands. You should now open a second terminal window and navigate to the `cmd/fetch.cli` directory and run `go build`. This builds the CLI tool that you can use to send commands to the Fetch service. Using the CLI, you can tell the Fetch service to retrieve a web page on your behalf, as follows:

```
./fetch.cli -u example.com
```

This can also be done with a simple JSON POST request to /fetch of the Fetch service. In Go, you would write something like the following code:

```go
package main

import (
  "bytes"
  "encoding/json"
  "fmt"
  "io/ioutil"
  "net/http"

  "github.com/slotix/dataflowkit/fetch"
)

func main() {
  r := fetch.Request{
    Type: "base",
    URL: "http://example.com",
    Method: "GET",
    UserToken: "randomString",
    Actions: "",
  }

  data, err := json.Marshal(&r)

  if err != nil {
    panic(err)
  }
  resp, err := http.Post("http://localhost:8000/fetch", "application/json",
bytes.NewBuffer(data))
  if err != nil {
    panic(err)
  }

  body, err := ioutil.ReadAll(resp.Body)
  if err != nil {
    panic(err)
  }

  fmt.Println(string(body))
}
```

The `fetch.Request` object is a convenient way of structuring our `POST` request data, and the `json` library makes it easy to attach as the request body. Most of the rest of the code you have already seen in earlier chapters. In this example, we use the basic type of fetcher which only uses HTTP requests. If we needed to drive a browser instead, we would be able to send actions to the browser in our request.

Actions are sent as an array of JSON objects representing a small subset of commands. As of right now, only the click and paginate commands are supported. If you want to send a `click` command to the browser, your Fetch request would look similar to the following example:

```
r := fetch.Request{
    Type: "chrome",
    URL: "http://example.com",
    Method: "GET",
    UserToken: "randomString",
    Actions: `[{"click":{"element":"a"}}]`,
}
```

By communicating with the external Fetch service, you can easily control the switch back and forth between HTTP requests and driving web browsers. Combined with the power of remote execution, you can make sure that you size the right machines for the right jobs.

The Parse service

The Parse service is responsible for parsing data out of an HTML page and returning it in an easily usable format, such as CSV, XML, or JSON. The Parse service relies on the Fetch service to retrieve the page, and does not function on its own. To get started using the Parse service, first navigate to your local repository and run `go build` from the `cmd/parse.d` directory. Once the build completes, you can start the service via `./parse.d`. There are many options you can set when configuring the Parse service that will determine the backend it uses to cache the results: how to handle pagination, the location of the Fetch service, and so on. For now, we will use the standard defaults.

To send commands to the Parse service, you use `POST` requests to the `/parse` endpoint. The body of the request contains information on what site to open, how to map HTML elements to fields and, and how to format the returned data. Let's look at the daily deals example from `Chapter 4`, *Parsing HTML*, and build a request for the Parse service. First, we will look at the `package` and `import` statements, as follows:

```
package main

import (
```

```
    "bytes"
    "encoding/json"
    "fmt"
    "io/ioutil"
    "net/http"

    "github.com/slotix/dataflowkit/fetch"
    "github.com/slotix/dataflowkit/scrape"
)
```

Here, you can see where we import the necessary `dataflowkit` packages. The `fetch` package is used in this example to build the request for the Parse service to send to the Fetch service. You can see it in the `main` function, as follows:

```
func main() {
  r := scrape.Payload{
    Name: "Daily Deals",
    Request: fetch.Request{
      Type: "Base",
      URL: "https://www.packtpub.com/latest-releases",
      Method: "GET",
    },
    Fields: []scrape.Field{
      {
        Name: "Title",
        Selector: `div.landing-page-row div[itemtype$="/Product"]
         div.book-block-title`,
        Extractor: scrape.Extractor{
          Types: []string{"text"},
          Filters: []string{"trim"},
        },
      }, {
        Name: "Price",
        Selector: `div.landing-page-row div[itemtype$="/Product"] div.book-
block-
        price-discounted`,
        Extractor: scrape.Extractor{
          Types: []string{"text"},
          Filters: []string{"trim"},
        },
      },
    },
    Format: "CSV",
  }
```

This `scrape.Payload` object is what we use to communicate with the Parse service. It defines the request to make to the Fetch service, as well as how to collect and format our data. In our case, we want to collect rows of two fields: the title and the price. We use CSS selectors to define where to find the fields, and where to extract the data from. The `Extractor` that this program will use is the text extractor which will copy all of the inner text for the matching element.

Finally, we send the request to the Parse service and wait for the result, as shown in the following example:

```
data, err := json.Marshal(&r)

if err != nil {
  panic(err)
}
resp, err := http.Post("http://localhost:8001/parse", "application/json",
bytes.NewBuffer(data))
if err != nil {
  panic(err)
}

body, err := ioutil.ReadAll(resp.Body)
if err != nil {
  panic(err)
}

fmt.Println(string(body))
}
```

The Parse service replies with a JSON object summarizing the whole process, including where we can find the file containing the results, as shown in the following example:

```
{
  "Output file":"results/f5ae68fa_2019-01-13_22:53.CSV",
  "Requests":{
    "initial":1
  },
  "Responses":1,
  "Task ID":"1Fk0qAso17vNnKpzddCyWUcVv6r",
  "Took":"3.209452023s"
}
```

The convenience that the Parse service offers, allows you as a user to be even more creative by building on top of it. With systems that are open source, and composable, you can start with a solid foundation and apply your best skills towards making a complete system. You are armed with enough knowledge and enough tools to build efficient and powerful systems, but I hope your learning does not stop here!

Summary

In this chapter, we looked under the hood at the components that make a solid web scraping system. We used `colly` to scrape HTML pages that did not require JavaScript. We used `chrome-protocol` to drive web browsers to scrape sites that do require JavaScript. Finally, we examined `dataflowkit` and saw how its architecture opens the door for building distributed web crawlers. There is more to learn and do when it comes to building distributed systems in Go, but this is where the scope of this book ends. I hope you check out some other publications on building applications in Go and continue to hone your skills!

Other Books You May Enjoy

If you enjoyed this book, you may be interested in these other books by Packt:

Python Web Scraping Cookbook
Michael Heydt

ISBN: 9781787285217

- Use a wide variety of tools to scrape any website and data—including BeautifulSoup, Scrapy, Selenium, and many more
- Master expression languages such as XPath, CSS, and regular expressions to extract web data
- Deal with scraping traps such as hidden form fields, throttling, pagination, and different status codes
- Build robust scraping pipelines with SQS and RabbitMQ
- Scrape assets such as images media and know what to do when Scraper fails to run
- Explore ETL techniques of build a customized crawler, parser, and convert structured and unstructured data from websites
- Deploy and run your scraper-as-aservice in AWS Elastic Container Service

R Web Scraping Quick Start Guide
Olgun Aydin

ISBN: 9781789138733

- Write and create regEX rules
- Write XPath rules to query your data
- Learn how web scraping methods work
- Use rvest to crawl web pages
- Store data retrieved from the web
- Learn the key uses of Rselenium to scrape data

Leave a review - let other readers know what you think

Please share your thoughts on this book with others by leaving a review on the site that you bought it from. If you purchased the book from Amazon, please leave us an honest review on this book's Amazon page. This is vital so that other potential readers can see and use your unbiased opinion to make purchasing decisions, we can understand what our customers think about our products, and our authors can see your feedback on the title that they have worked with Packt to create. It will only take a few minutes of your time, but is valuable to other potential customers, our authors, and Packt. Thank you!

Index

P

Parse service 111, 113
proxy
  about 76
  dedicated proxy 77
  in Go 79
  public proxy 77
  shared proxy 77
public proxy
  about 77
  reference 77

R

race conditions 88, 90
regexp package
  links, searching 52
  prices, searching 53
  used, for searching 51
robots.txt file 33, 34, 35

S

search
  with Cascading Style Sheets (CSS) 57
  with regexp package 51
  XPath queries, using 54
Secure Copy Protocol (SCP) 76
shared proxy 77
strings package
  doctype, checking 50
  links, counting 49
  used, for searching 49
sync package helpers
  about 94

atomic counters 96
conditions 94, 96

T

transport object 79

U

User-Agent string
  about 36
  example 36, 38

V

Virtual Private Network (VPN) 80, 81
Virtual Private Server (VPS) 75, 76

W

web scraper
  datasets, building 7, 8
  need for 6
  price comparison 7
  search engines 6
  throttling 38, 39, 40, 41
web scraping
  about 5, 6
  components 99
  with Go 8
whitelisting 81

X

XPath queries
  daily deals, scrapping 54, 55
  products, collecting 56
  used, for searching 54

Made in the USA
Monee, IL
23 February 2021

61198322R00077